St Brigid
& Other Amazing Irish Women

LORRAINE MULHOLLAND from Co. Antrim studied at Queen's University, Belfast. She studied Zoology for one year, then Divinity for three years (B.D. Hons, 1st). She was a Secondary School teacher, head of Religious Education and also taught History, Geography, and Personal & Social Education. On Twitter she is *Irish History Bitesize!* (@lorraineelizab6). On Instagram she is @lorraineelizabeth59.

MATTHEW JACKSON is an animation student from Co. Antrim, currently studying a bachelors degree at Dundee University. He works as a freelance painter and illustrator (Instagram @mtthwjcksn_arts), and his work was exhibited in the Ulster Museum at the age of 18. Matthew's keen interest in history and pop culture is blended in his work, adding a contemporary feel to the ancient stories told in these pages.

SAINT BRIGID
& Other Amazing Irish Women

WRITTEN BY

LORRAINE MULHOLLAND

ILLUSTRATED BY

MATTHEW JACKSON

columba
BOOKS

FOR JOEL NATHAN MULHOLLAND
my amazing son

First published in 2023 by Columba Books
Block 3b, Bracken Business Park,
Bracken Road, Sandyford, Dublin 18, D18 K277
www.columbabooks.com

© 2023 Lorraine Mulholland
Illustrations by Matthew Jackson

ISBN: 978-1-78218-405-8

Set in FreightText Pro 11/14 and King Victory
Book and cover design by Alba Esteban | Alestura Design

Printed with L&C, Poland

Contents

About This Book

A book of amazing wonder saints,
I ask you what image that really paints?
Is praying, fasting and healing boring?
Well, these gals sure won't leave you snoring!

At least 150 Irish kingdoms at a time,
So many kickass princesses in this rhyme
But they didn't want power and riches,
At unexpected moments they'll leave you in stitches!

Holy girls, set apart, with difference,
Don't they have any sense?!
Causing wonder and enjoyment,
From God they were sent.

Women who didn't marry,
But long did they tarry,
Over poor, sick and weary,
Even dragons didn't make them teary!

Heroines who were shocking,
Though druids gave them a mocking,
Over 343 Irish ladies,
One even called down rabies!

Many animals get a mention,
And with kings there's tension,
Fox, deer, boar, cow, bird,
God's message too they heard!

Storms, and walking on water,
No sight of an ordinary daughter!
Soaring angels, from heaven too,
While suitors tried to woo

Girls of power and prophecy,
On a leaf one sailed the sea!
Twenty-three stories to read again,
Who's in your top ten?

Lots of facts, faith and some folklore,
Unusual tales that make you want more,
Even a surprising mermaid is in these pages,
I hope you'll read this book for ages!

An encyclopaedia of horrid histories,
Pulling out eyes, and God's mysteries,
Many cephalophores carrying their head,
They praised the Lord when supposed to be dead!

To England, Scotland, Belgium and Gaul,
They didn't let distance block like a wall,
Beyond Ireland's shores they travelled the earth,
Bringing good news, true mirth and rebirth!

There's many memories of saints all around,
Statues, wells, and church windows I've found,
Names of sports teams, ships, planes, and a tea!
They're so important that's easy to see.

Currachs and Culdees, crosiers and bells,
Chalices and chasubles, patens and wells,
Calderas and nocturns, a new set of words,
Go to the glossary for those you've not heard!

Write poems, draw art, think deep,
Let saints' stories and Bible verses meet,
Then in the quiz check what you know,
And the answers page will show!

A book of amazing wonder women,
I hope you give it ten out of ten!
I pray this book speaks their story,
and gives them and God the glory.

Y ou might have heard that Ireland is known as the 'land of saints and scholars'. Well, this is a book of twenty-three stories about Irish female saints. I have also listed 343 names of Irish female saints in the 'Wonder Women' chapter towards the back. I hope you find this book to be like a mini-encyclopaedia.

Do you like princesses? Then this might be the book for you! There are many, many princesses in this book. You see, Ireland was made up of a huge number of kingdoms ('túatha' in Irish). Dr. Mícheál Ó Mainnín told me that a famous historian of early Ireland, F.J. Byrne (d. 2017), reckoned that 'there were probably no less than 150 kings in the country at any given date between the fifth and twelfth centuries.' And if each 'king' had more than one daughter, then that's far more than 150 princesses at any one time! But the princesses in this book are different. They had wealth and position to spread their new faith of Christianity.

Do you like horrible, gruesome history? Long, long ago, before the monks recorded Ireland's history and stories, there were myths and legends of gods and goddesses and many other strange visitors to Ireland's shores. Back then, the leaders of Ireland's religion were the pagan druids, highly esteemed in society. They did not take kindly to their faith being ousted from the position of top religion and neither did many of their followers. You will read shocking, gruesome stories about what happened to some of the saints because of this. You will also learn what a 'cephalophore' is!

Are you interested in folklore? You will hear old names such as Caer, Brigid, Manannán mac Lir, the Cailleach, Fionn MacCumhaill (Finn McCool), Cú Chulainn, Balor of the Evil Eye, the Salmon of Knowledge, and the merrow. You will learn about how sometimes our saints had to relate their Christian teachings to people raised on the old stories of these gods, heroes and magical creatures. They were clever girls and women to make their teaching relevant. It wasn't just St Patrick who did that by preaching at the Hill of Tara in Co. Meath – the capital of the High King of Ireland.

What about pirates, dragons and mermaids? They're here too! Do you like animals? This book is a Noah's ark of animals, but with a difference. Super-hero bees, a seriously scary snake, a magical otter, elusive white deer, two lovable donkeys, birds under God's control, an astonishing cuckoo, an amazing pet fox and an extremely strange stag beetle. And that's just some of them!

Heroism comes in all shapes and sizes. Our saints in this book are often very different to each other, but they are all outstanding and extraordinary heroines. They are amazing Irish women who lived such impressive lives that we still remember and celebrate them today. I hope you find the adjective I have given them helpful. They were not randomly chosen; each tries to communicate the most important thing about that saint.

Are the stories true? Well, some are more 'stories of faith' and some have lots of folklore thrown in. In each one, I have tried to stay true to the essence of the original story.

I hope you enjoy the facts. There are signs of saints all around us still today. Not just in holy wells and church windows, but in the names given to sports teams, aeroplanes, boats, streets, schools and even a brand of tea (to mention just a few).

I also hope you enjoy the Irish words. I am learning some Irish, so have included some of the words that I have learned. You should note however that it is modern Irish used, except where I've specifically said it's Old Irish. For most words, we don't know what they would have been in the early medieval period. But don't let that spoil the stories!

If you like the introductory poem, you will enjoy the fun 'task' I've assigned after each story. Look out for questions, poetry, story writing, gardening, baking, map reading, embroidery, flower picking, library research, and arts and craft challenges.

Astounding Attracta

ISSSSS. . . It was a gorgeous sun-kissed day at Monasteraden village, Clogher, in Co. Sligo. But unknown to a girl called Attracta (or Athracht), the meanest, deadliest snake in all of Ireland (and the world) was watching her from 100 metres (230 ft) away.

It had super sight from its huge, hellish black eyes. Even though it was a hot day, it could sense Attracta's approach by using its super sense of temperature awareness. The heat sensors on its head told it Attracta's body temperature was warmer than the grass, trees and stones around her, so it had another way of 'seeing' her. It also had an astounding sense of smell. It flicked its long, forked tongue in and out to taste Attracta's scent. So, it knew in several ways that Attracta was about to walk towards it. 'Sss-surely this girl will make a fine meal for my sss-stomach! I will teach her a lesssss-on!' said that serpent.

This monstrosity of a beast was no ordinary snake ('Nathair Nimhe' in Irish). Indeed, it had traits of many of the scariest killer serpents from around the world. It weighed over 100 kilograms, just like a green anaconda from South America (the heaviest snake in the world). It was about 7 metres (23 ft) long, like the longest reticulated python ever found (the longest snake in the world). How this got to Co. Sligo when it should have been in South or Southeast Asia is beyond me!

What made it look even more seriously sinister was that, despite its weight, it raised the top third of its body up into the air, like a king cobra (the world's longest venomous snake, also from South and Southeast Asia). It was a *huge* mass of coils, with its neck flapped wide out to form a hood-shape...much wider than a normal king cobra! It was a creature never seen on earth before, never mind in Ireland.

Now, you might interrupt this story and say, 'Surely St Patrick drove all the snakes out of Ireland?' Now, everyone knows that, but there is one particularly troublesome female serpent who proved a little tricky. She was called the Fire Spitter ('Caoránach' in Irish) and was said to be the Devil's mother. St Patrick chased her all the way from Croagh Patrick in Co. Mayo to Co. Sligo (and on into Co. Donegal in another version of the story). All along the way, that awful serpent spat in the wells. However, she was no match for St Patrick and soon she was banished. So, we don't know how it happened, but it seems that there were a few snake escapees and this monster, like the Fire Spitter, must have been one of them.

It puffed and hissed, lunging back and forth, but was still hidden from Attracta because of the trees. Slithering around now, it made an S-shape as it spat and raged. The snake you see had been eating up the villagers' hens and pigs. Even some young lambs and calves seemed to have disappeared. One villager thought that he had seen a monstrously long creature down by the edge of the farms. He had also seen lots of animal bones. Rumours were rife about it and they knew something needed to be done. One villager had bravely snuck down at a distance from the creature's outline and shouted, 'We're going to get the girl called Attracta to deal with you!' The snake was livid with anger, but the people prayed and sent word to Attracta. They had heard she was from God. Perhaps God would use her to help them. Though, what would a girl do against a monster?

As Attracta walked closer towards the place where the villagers suspected the creature was, she kept praying herself. Now she could see the massive outline of its body. 'I know who you are, Attracta, I'm not sss-scared of you,' it hissssed. 'I'm sss-SO going to gobble you up!' At this, Attracta knew the snake was no ordinary animal but a demonic creature that should not be roaming the Earth. Perhaps it had only temporarily taken the form of a snake. Again, now that Attracta was nearly within striking distance, it opened its scaly mouth to expose its hissing fangs. Attracta could easily see its record-breaking 5 centimetres (2 inch) fangs, just like those of a Gaboon viper from Africa! It then spat and slobbered out some noxious, sulphurous-smelling fluid (like a pine snake from North America). Thankfully, Attracta was still at a safe distance from it.

'Ooh Attracta, I'm ssss-alivating at the thought of squeezing you to death and sss-striking into your skin with my poissss-onous venom.' If it had the most poisonous venom in the world, then it was even more dangerous than an Inland Taipan from Australia! 'I'm jusss-t about to lay some eggs-sss, so that my children can sss-strike fear into even more of you humans-ssss!' It then rattled the end of its tail, just like a North American diamond-backed rattlesnake. What an oddly terrifying creature it was! What do YOU think is the ssss-scariest thing about this serpent?

Anyone else but Attracta would have been stunned and frozen to the spot, stupefied with fear. But this girl was special and she was not scared. This snake was just being *silly* now...and anyway, it talked too much. While it was speaking (or should I say, ssss-speaking), Attracta ran towards it, not batting an eyelid. She lunged herself forward (as the snake had been doing previously), trusting God to protect her and guide the movements of her hands, and swung her staff (which all good church leaders had). She swiped its raised hood of a neck to the side with the staff, then crashed down on its fat, long body, some distance back from its head. Now, Attracta had felt God saying to her to sharpen the end of her staff before she came to Clogher, so she had. And so her staff went right through the monster's skin when she pierced its body. AND it turned out, unbeknown to Attracta, she had in fact pierced right through its heart!

At the place where Attracta's staff pierced through the heart and its body a holy well erupted from the ground. Along the top of the well are thirteen water-worn stones, known locally as 'the serpent's eggs', as it is believed they might be that snake's eggs hardened into stone. Many people say the thirteen stones symbolise Jesus and the twelve Apostles. Over the centuries, this well was used by women who wanted to have children. A woman would take one of the stones from the well and, after her child was born, return it. Nowadays, the stones are cemented into the wall behind the well. This wall has five cross slabs, which are very worn now, and one of them has a crucifixion scene. There is also a bullaun at this well, which is a small hollow in a boulder. The water in this stone was believed to cure children who had rickets. Rickets is a condition that results in weak, soft bones in children because of a lack of vitamin D and certain minerals.

And so, it turned out that a scary snake was no match for an even greater and more astounding girl, called Attracta. But that is not the end of the story. Let us go back in time to when Attracta was a young child. Many years before, when she was little, Attracta would have the strangest dreams while asleep in her bed. They weren't just about killing that serpent, but about telling people the future, looking after the poor and the ill, parting a way through a huge lake, and even battling an even scarier creature...! She wondered what Caer, the Irish goddess of sleep and dreams, might be saying to her. But then, not long after this, she became a Christian. She realised that her dreams were from God, not the pagan goddess Caer. Attracta never forgot those dreams, and she pondered them often. This is the rest of Attracta's story. She did some amazing, shocking and brave things. Let's see if the other dreams Attracta had ever came true! Do you think they will?

Now, we don't know much about Attracta's childhood. There is some disagreement about which family Attracta was actually from. There is a tradition belief that she was from Co. Sligo, but scholars think she was from Ulster in the north of Ireland. There are three men from Ulster who could be her father – Talán, Sárán and Tigernach from the Cenél nEógain. I like to think of them as Talán the Terrible, Sárán the Strong, and Tigernach the Truthful. But I'm just guessing. We also don't know which religion her parents followed. They might have been Christians. Or they might have been pagans who followed the druid religion. The druids taught about the Tuatha Dé Danann. They were the Irish gods and goddesses of the tribe of Dana. Caer, who they believed gave dreams, was one of those goddesses.

We might not know who her father was, but we do think that Attracta had two brothers, both of whom became monks. One was Cóemán of Ardcavan, Co. Wexford. He was once the servant of the Queen of Leinster. Her other brother (who shared the same mother) was called Conall, and among his churches he became the patron of Drum, the original parish church of Boyle in Co. Roscommon. So, since her brothers were Christians, there is a good chance that Attracta grew up in a Christian home.

From childhood, Attracta showed that she heard from God. Not only did she have detailed and unusual dreams (like Joseph in the Bible), but she had the gift of prophecy. This meant she heard messages from God. One day, Attracta had run past the idea to her brother Conall that she would like to lead a church near him some day. But Conall wasn't impressed with that idea and sent another female saint to try to persuade her never to do that. Well, Attracta prayed and heard God speak. She told her brother Conall that his church, and one other, would be reduced to poverty. She explained that God had shown her that a third monastery would take over from them. And...it happened just as Attracta said!

When barely a teenager, before her monster-battling days, Attracta didn't want to marry. This was much to her father's displeasure, who wanted her to marry even though she was probably only twelve or thirteen. She was described as beau-

14

tiful, with several suitors, but Attracta would have none of it. She had heard that St Patrick was in Connacht (the province in west Ireland), in what is now the barony of Coolavin in south Co. Sligo. So, off she set to hear St Patrick. She took her maid, Mitain, and a male servant called Mochain. It was a long journey. When they got there, Attracta and Mitain were delighted when St Patrick bestowed the veil upon them both (that meant they both became nuns). While St Patrick was dedicating them to Christ, an actual veil fell from heaven, which St Patrick gave to Attracta. Of course, she felt she was not good enough and suggested giving it to Mitain, but St Patrick insisted on putting it upon Attracta's head. It is said Attracta wore that veil until the day she died.

Huge numbers of churches, monasteries and convents can trace their origins back to St Patrick and Killaraght, 'church of Attracta' as it came to be called, was no exception. It was close to where they were, at Lough Techet (now called Lough Gara). St Patrick decided that St Attracta was perfect to lead the convent as Abbess. Other young girls and women joined her there. St Patrick is also said to have left a paten, chalice and cross with Attracta. Some say that cross was the distinctive Irish high cross, with the top of the cross through a circle (representing the pagan symbol of the sun, which had been worshipped). Another time, a chasuble is said to have fallen from heaven for her, but she did not feel she was good enough for this special garment and, of course, chose to give it away.

Attracta had always wanted to set up a hospice (or hospital); a home of sorts for those who were poor travellers, strangers and the ill. She had always felt that way, so it seemed obvious to her that it was God's plan. Also, it clearly said in the Bible to do things to show that your faith in God is real:

> *As the body without the spirit is dead, so faith without deeds is dead.*
> – James 2:26, NIV

☞ *Can you understand what this Bible verse means?*

✤ ✤ ✤

And so, Attracta told Mochain, her male servant, all about what she hoped for. Mochain went out early one spring morning, just as the sun was starting to dawn, to find a good location for the hospice. Out he walked into the woods that March morning. He loved the sounds of the forest...animals and birds everywhere. Ill people would certainly feel better out here in nature, he thought. Then, before Mochain even realised that the dawn chorus of birdsong had made him distracted from his search, there was a 'hop, hop, hop' and a whole husk of hares bounded past! That was unusual, as there were so many and they often preferred to be out in the fields rather than in the forest. Indeed, Mochain knew that their name in Irish was 'Giorria' or 'Mìl Maige', meaning 'Animal of the Plains/Open Spaces'. Mochain thought hard about the hares. They were extremely significant in Irish folklore, you see. So long as the hares weren't fairies about to take him to the Otherworld, then it was probably a good omen to see one, never mind a 'husk', 'drove' or 'down' of them. In folklore it was often interesting to see where a hare might lead you. So, Mochain followed the racing hares.

SUDDENLY... Mochain looked up and saw the *perfect* location for the hospice! It was in a clearing in the woods. Mochain smiled to himself. That was why he'd seen the hares. Mochain believed that God, who is in charge of all creatures (including these hares), was perhaps leading him to this open space. It was, by the way, the sort of location they are usually seen in. Then, Mochain had an even bigger smile on his face. He wandered into the clearing and looked around carefully and intently. There, around the edge of the trees, he realised there were little paths or roads coming into the clearing. He started to count, 'One, two, three, four...' My oh my, he thought, can there be more? He continued, 'Five, six, seven...thanks be to God in heaven!' There were *seven* roads coming out of the forest to meet in that exact spot!

Surely, Attracta, Mitain and himself would come upon *many* travellers at this spot, since there were seven roads? Lots of roads meant lots of people. And so, Mochain rushed back to Attracta. He fell on his knees with his arms up in the air, nearly too excited to speak. Attracta was delighted at the news. She prayed and her idea about the hospice became clearer. She got permission from the local lord to use the clearing in the woods. Then she gave that tract of land to Mochain and put him in charge. Mochain would lead the hospice for her. Attracta became known throughout the area for her virtue of hospitality. And, do you know, Killaraght survived as a hospital for the poor until 1539 (during the reign of King Henry VIII, who shut down all the monasteries).

Another day, Attracta showed that she was like the Old Testament prophet Moses. Some locals had been taken captive in battle and were being held as hostages. The chiefs of Leyny in Co. Sligo forced the King of Connacht to return them. However, the King must have changed him mind, as after the men of Leyny rescued their men from his castle, the King's soldiers chased them towards the shore of Lough Gara. Like Moses and the Israelites with the Pharaoh's Egyptian army hot on their tail at the Red Sea, they reached the lough. They were hemmed in with enemy soldiers behind and on either side! A messenger was quickly sent to Attracta who was nearby in Boyle. The message begged her to come to their aid. Off Attracta set and prayed. As it happened for the Israelites, so the deep waters divided. *Splash*, went the lough loudly at her feet. Two walls of water formed either side of Attracta. And so, the men of Leyny passed over on dry land. Can you imagine what it must have looked like? I wonder if they saw the fish in the water that was raised up like waterfalls on each side of them.

Attracta ordered that no one was to look behind while crossing. But while crossing, a bard named Feolan (who told stories and songs) was drowned! But, of course, he was brought back to life by the prayers of Attracta. This man afterwards devoted his life to the service of God and died a saint. It is also said that Attracta built a ford (a causeway or raised crossing) across Lough Gara and a house for people crossing to stay in.

Another day, a local king of a small kingdom in that part of Connacht, called King Keannfaelaid, decided that he was going to build a castle. This idea had come from his rather haughty chiefs, who felt that their king should have the most magnificent castle erected in order to show off the kingdom to everyone else. Now, this king passed an edict saying he wanted everyone, including Attracta, to help him. Well, to cut a long story short, Attracta received the edict by letter, after which she went to the King and said, 'No!' But since she was kind, she offered to bring him things that he'd need, using her saint abilities of course! The King wasn't impressed, but Attracta set off to get wood to build with from a nearby forest, with St Nath Í and some servants and horses. But the poor horses were rather old and tired, and it turned out they just weren't up to the job. Having two Christian leaders there, of course, they ended up using some wild deer to pull the cart full of timber!

But then another problem appeared. The rope fastening the wood broke and they didn't have any more with them. But it is said that Attracta smartly used some strands of her long, silky hair to replace the rope. Miraculously, the wood was held in place until they delivered the timber to the very ungrateful king. In fact, the King and Queen, who were obviously not Christian believers, were so enraged that they tried to set the town dogs on the deer and tear them to pieces! Attracta loved animals, but she prayed that the royal horses would temporarily become so mad that they would kill those dangerous dogs. Instead of the deer being killed, any townspeople who had set the dogs on the deer were all trodden down by the King's horses or even torn to pieces by their very own dogs! The story continues that the tamed deer licked the bottom of Attracta's clothes, then safely returned to their forest, having done their job. Attracta then told the horrid king that God had told her he and his sons would lose their kingdom (and it happened as she said). What became of the King's horses and the dangerous dogs? Well, the horses became sane again (it wasn't their fault after all) and legend records that the dogs were turned to stone.

Attracta accomplished so much in her life. Not only did she start a hospital, part the waters of Lough Gara, battle a huge dangerous serpent, and deal with a nasty obnoxious king, she also killed another, even more monstrous beast! A dragon. The dragon of Glennawoo. It lived in a hill called Brumas, at the foot of the Ox mountains in what is now Layny barony. This dragon was not a good dragon (as is often the case in stories from eastern countries like China). No, this dragon was gruesomely dangerous! Not only did it kill all the farm animals and wildlife, it ate people. And like most dragons in the west, it breathed fire.

Its back had a grassy-green hue to it, meaning it was impossible to see whenever it landed. It had long hair flowing down its back, like a horse's mane. It had a distinctive, blue tummy underneath. The blue meant that, again, it was nearly impossible to see when it soared down from a cloudless sky on sunny days. Like most reptiles, it would come out to warm itself more often on summer days. Its head was a fawn-brown and its long teeth were sharper than those of a wild boar! The eyes were an unearthly yellow that made it look unlike anything in the animal kingdom that was native to Ireland.

One summer, when the dragon was out and about pillaging more than usual, the local king, King Bec, sent messengers to where Attracta was staying. It was a very desperate sort of message, as you can imagine. The people who lived in that part of the kingdom near the dragon were in obvious despair. Before Attracta set off, she fasted and prayed. This monster sounded far worse than the scary snake she'd faced a short time before. The dragon was so large that whenever it went to Lough Talt for a drink and fish supper, its tail stayed in its cave under Brumas. Lough Talt was about a ten-minute walk (for humans) to the northeast – that shows how huge this dragon was!

On the day that Attracta encountered it, the dragon rubbed his humongous blue tummy and thought to himself, 'What shall I eat today?' Off he set to Lough Talt. He was thirsty, so he drank down nearly all the lake! Then he set about eating. He opened his huge mouth, just like a basking shark (but *much* bigger), then went up and down the lough, jaws agape, scooping up everything he could eat. Brown trout, mouthfuls and mouthfuls of stickleback, arctic char, eel, and white-clawed crayfish. There was no way *that* was enough, so he lashed out with his ginormous claws and swiped some beautiful swans, ducks, dippers and vast numbers of various types of gulls. A quick blast from his nostrils and he ate them roasted. Then with a loud burp, he exclaimed, 'Delicious!' Basically, he ate all the wildlife at Lough Talt!

He was just about to return to his cave in the hill for a snooze (before another trip out to eat some farm animals) when *boom!* he felt a shockwave of energy hit his tail! He cried in agony. *Boom!* Attracta hit the dragon with her staff again. It was like a seismic wave from an earthquake. *Crash*, went the dragon's tail up, up through the roof of the cave! The cave roof came thundering down. That is why, even to this day, we cannot find its cave in Co. Sligo. The dragon flew up into the air, turned back from Lough Talt, and came back towards Attracta. As you'd expect, his sharp incisors gleamed and his fire-filled nostrils flared. He roared like a lion. The smell of yellow stinking sulphur came out of his throat. But my, did he halt with a crash when he saw her! You didn't expect that...or did you?

There was a short, tense pause when it might have seemed uncertain what was going to happen. Some say he bit down on Attracta's staff, which she had held out at him...and that was how he was killed – as soon as Attracta's staff entered his mouth. But I think Attracta didn't need to do that. I say it was with one steely gaze from Attracta's fiery eyes that the power of God in her killed that dragon stone-cold dead. Then, in the very same spot where she had crashed down on his tail at the cave, a beautiful spring-well sprang up. It is the same well that is there today. There is a sign of the cross marked onto its wall and people from all over come there to visit, especially in July and August, and pray to St Barbara there. That dragon of Glennawoo was truly killed.

Though the Annals of Ulster in 735 AD (about 200 years after Attracta lived) say, 'A huge dragon was seen with great thunder after it, at the end of autumn.' Also, in 746 AD, it is recorded that, somewhere in Ireland, 'dragons were seen in the sky'. Were they dragons or were they maybe meteors? What do you think?

Which part of Attracta's astounding story do you like the best?

TASK

Make your own scariest snake or deadly dragon with random materials, like kitchen rolls and cardboard egg cartons. Make sure you colour and decorate them!

DID YOU KNOW?

- *Feast Days:* 11th August (main), 9th February and 6th January (not celebrated anymore).

- *Other names:* Athracht, Attracht, Araght, Atty, Arata, and Tarachta (or Tarahata in other countries).

- Attracta also seemed to have led a church at Drum, not far from Boyle, Co. Roscommon (later named Drumconell, as her brother Conall was in leadership there too).

- In 2019, Aer Lingus named the aeroplane Airbus A321LR 'St Attracta'.

- There are lots of schools named after her too, e.g. in Tubbercurry, Co. Sligo; Ballaghaderreen, Co. Roscommon; Charlestown, Co. Mayo, and two in Dublin.

- Most species of snake are harmless to humans, but venomous ones kill more than 20,000 people a year. (Have a read of *The Animal Book: A Visual Encyclopedia of Life on Earth* to learn more). Some people have given even higher estimates!

- Fr. Liam Swords wrote that eight parishes in total have holy wells dedicated to St Attracta. In Co. Mayo, there are wells at Tample near Charlestown, Killasser (destroyed) and Attymass. Also, in Co. Sligo there are wells at Clogher (Monasteraden), Glennawoo, Kilfree, Killaraght, Kilmactigue (forgotten), Kilturra, Gurteen (forgotten) and Tobercurry. If you live in this area, perhaps you could try to locate some of Attracta's wells?

Bega & her Bracelet

'Bega! Bega! Wake up, dear girl, I have a gift for you!' Bega stirred awake and rubbed her tired eyes. Who was this before her? A bright light shone everywhere in Bega's bedroom; it was an angel who was speaking. The angel continued, 'I have been sent to instruct you to leave your father's home, Bega. You must get into a boat journeying across the Irish Sea immediately. I also have a gift for you.'

You're probably wondering, who was Bega and what was the gift? Bega was a beautiful Irish princess who was pledged in marriage to a pagan Viking prince from Norway, far to the north of Ireland. She had been in quite a dilemma recently, since that prince didn't follow Christianity. That was one reason she didn't want to marry him – the other reason was that she wanted to stay single and become a nun. She had prayed for this, and now this angel was speaking to her, guiding her to flee across the Irish Sea. Can you guess what the gift from the angel was...?

It was a bracelet! A very special gift. 'Thank you so much, kind angel,' said Bega. The angel told her exactly where to find the boat, and with that Bega's adventure began. However, there is a saying that God works in mysterious ways. On the way eastward, the waves in the Irish Sea swelled up and up, higher and higher, until the boat Bega was in was thrown over and capsized upside down. And so, Bega's boat was shipwrecked on its route to England. But thankfully this happened not that far from England's coast. Bega and the others on board were able to cling onto pieces of wood from the wreckage and swim towards the shore. Taking the location of where she washed up on land as a sign, Bega stayed at the place that would one day be named after her: St Bees in Cumbria (just south of Whitehaven, in the area of Copeland). Bee is another way that you can spell Bega's name.

Indeed, Bega performed many great miracles. Here is the story of the nine that are traditionally told about Bega (the first one was the angel giving her the bracelet).

After that, the second miracle happened, while she was still young. It was just after she had arrived in Cumbria, when she was living alone as a hermit (which means spending a lot of time alone). She didn't yet have a group of other Christians in a community of nuns to reply on for basic necessities like food. She drank each day from a clear spring of water, but didn't have bread. So, as you can imagine, it was quite challenging for Bega! Nevertheless, she prayed on the Bible verse below and asked God to provide her with real bread:

> Then Jesus declared, 'I am the bread of life. Whoever comes to me will never
> go hungry, and whoever believes in me will never be thirsty.'
> – John 6:35, NIV

But one day, as she was sitting on the grass near the sea, she heard a *caw caw*! It was a crow. Then, a *tic* sound from a robin. A chorus of birdsong continued. *Chiff-chaff, chiff-chaff, chiff-chiff-chaff*, from a chiffchaff. *Hoo-eet* – a willow warbler! *Pink, pink*, went a chaffinch. *Ttsip*, called a song thrush as it flew towards Bega. As each arrived, Bega was astounded to see each one drop a morsel or two of bread or cheese at her feet! Where they found this food, Bega did not know. *Twit-twit-twit-twit* and a slower *sirr-sirr-sirr* came from a nuthatch.

Bega was *so* happy at this food, obviously sent from God, that she exclaimed: 'Thank you so much! I can't believe there's even cheese with the bread!' Then a funny, cheeky yellowhammer said to her, 'Little-bit-of-bread-and-no-cheeeeese!' (But then, if you know yellowhammers, they say that to everyone). And so it continued, on and on until Bega's tummy was quite full. Each day for a time, until Bega got to know more people, who would give her food too, she relied on these feathered friends. Blackbirds, bullfinches, blue tits, greenfinches, house and tree sparrows, goldfinches, little wrens, herons, wood pigeons, buzzards – *so* many birds – both large and small. This miracle was called 'the miracle of the birds'. Like with the Old Testament prophet, Elijah, birds had miraculously brought Bega food. Elijah was fed bread and meat by ravens twice a day (see 1 Kings 17:2-6 in the Bible). On the last day of this miracle, a little great tit said to her, *Tea-cher, tea-cher, tea-cher*. It was like a secret message to Bega. Can you understand it? Bega knew that God was saying to her she was ready to be a teacher to people, to teach them about God and His ways.

In the following months, Bega became more and more sure that she was ready to start a convent for other girls and women. But there was one problem. A local stingy lord, called Lord Egremont, laughed at her idea. You see, she needed him to provide some land to her so she could build a convent for her community. He was a horrid man and he had no plans to give away any of his land. He was quite sarcastic, as well as generally rude, so he promised her, 'Girl, I will give you as much land as snow will cover tomorrow'. The reason he said that was because the next day was Midsummer Day (24th June). That proud landowner didn't expect it to snow in the summer at all. But Bega had faith and replied, 'Excellent, you've got a deal! But you must stick to your promise'. And you'll never believe it, but what should happen? As silently as could be, a huge snowstorm fell. Down fluttered the snow in beautiful, huge flakes, each one unique. It was *snowing*! It snowed so much that it was white for 3 miles around where Bega lived. The laughing Lord Egrement had to keep his promise and Bega built a dwelling place for her nuns. Things were going well!

Indeed, things went extremely well for Bega and her nuns. But as time progressed, there was an argument. You see, some of Bega's neighbours had been coming on to her lands without permission. If trespassing was the only issue, it wouldn't have been too bad. But no, they had *taken* some of it. They were *stealing* her land! Bega prayed and asked God to do something about it. God had given the land, so surely He would help. *Flutter flutter*, came the flakes of snow again. Bega looked outside and thought to herself, 'Oh my goodness, a second snow miracle is happening!' This time, there was no snow at Bega's convent, but there were fields and fields deep with it all around Bega's land. God, you see, was showing everyone that *He* knew where the boundary of Bega's land was, and that He wanted it to stay there. God did *not* like stealing. After this, that awful landlord had some faith in Bega and allowed her to keep the land he had given her, and he made the thieves leave the area. So, this miracle of snow was the fourth that Bega experienced.

The years and decades passed, and things went well at Bega's convent. Until one day, a young man from Galloway in Scotland decided to steal a horse from them. The young man's mum tried to persuade him not to do it and warned him that God's punishment would follow, but that cheeky boy stuck out his bottom, rubbed it in in a very rude way and said, 'What can this little old woman do to me?' He laughed, pointing at his bottom, and said, 'Here, here she will shoot me!' That silly boy got his judgement. Bega had been praying, you see. Later that day, as he was stealing one of the horses, some of the villagers shot his bottom full of *lots* of painful arrows. It happened just as he had said!

Another day, Bega looked out the window. *Clip-clop*, *clip-clop*, went the sound of hooves outside. Some men from Godard of Millom (another rich landowner) had decided to graze their horses on Bega's land. Those horses were eating all of Bega's good grass, which she needed for her own livestock. The men pretended not to notice what their horses were doing. Time for prayer again! Bega liked animals, but when it came time for the men to saddle the horses, they found the hooves looked strange. They looked as if they were about to fall off! But, of course, it was just an illusion to scare the men. The poor horses were completely fine. Bega would never harm an animal. After that encounter with Bega, Godard of Millom never allowed his men to venture onto her land again. In fact, he repented and gave one of his fields to the convent. A strange detail is that, after some of those horses died of old age, some of their hooves were hung up in the convent church for many years after. Are you keeping track of what miracle number that is? That was miracle number six!

A different day, a very sad thing happened. Three men had been drinking too much alcohol and had become drunk. Since they didn't realise what they were doing, they had very accidentally killed a fourth man who had been with them. We don't know the details, but it was definitely an accident. In Egremont Castle jail, they were full of remorse and repented. 'Please forgive us, God!' they wailed and cried. 'We are so sorry for our sin!' They prayed and prayed. Having heard about the great St Bega, they prayed to her also, asking for help from her. Low and behold, the story is that Bega miraculously appeared in their prison cell as if in a vision, miraculously spiriting them away to her convent. They lived happily with her and her nuns for a long time after that.

The eighth miracle tells of two sick brothers. One of the boys couldn't walk and the other had a terrible ulcer. Their father, who was from France, saw a vision in the town of Tynmouth. Maybe it predicted a great healing? Maybe God told him to travel to Bega? He told his boys about the vision and immediately they piped up, 'Oh Father, can we go see Bega? Perhaps she can help us!' One son said, 'I'd so love to run and play with my friends like the other boys.' The other added, 'I'd so like to feel well, Father, and not have this pain and bleeding in my stomach.' Tynmouth is in Northumberland, which is on the opposite coast of England, so they had a long journey ahead. The father took his boys to St Bees in a cart and, of course, they were healed! They were so thankful to Bega that they left her the cart as a thank you.

The ninth traditional miracle ascribed to Bega happened in her chapel, in 1313. The sight of a blind Irish boy was recovered.

So, you might wonder, what became of Bega's bracelet? For many years, it was kept at her convent. It was said that many miracles happened near this relic. In the Middle Ages, there was a custom to take oaths on it. This practice still existed in the thirteenth century!

What do you think St Bega's bracelet looked like?

What do you think St Bega's bracelet looked like? Have a go at designing it the way it might have been. Or, if you want to be even more adventurous, design a modern bracelet for Bega!

DID YOU KNOW?

- **Feast Days:** 7th November (main), 6th September, 31st October and 17th December (not celebrated anymore).

- **Other names:** Bee, Beya, Begh.

- St Bega's Way is a 36-mile walk between two of the churches dedicated to Bega. You either walk it in three days (going east) or run it as a marathon in one day (going west). People like to think about where Bega would have walked. And the countryside is beautiful! It is a pilgrimage for some, to remember her.

- The Priory Church of St Mary and St Bega (Church of England) in St Bees has a special service to celebrate Bega on St Bega's Eve (6th November). Activities have included children taking flowers to the outstretched arms of their statue of St Bega. This also happens on Midsummer's Day. They have also sung the hymn to St Bega that was used by the monks in St Bees.

- Some people believe that when Bega was an old lady, fearing Viking raiders, she moved further inland to Northumbria.

- There are similar stories about St Begnet of Dalkey Island, Dublin.

Bountiful Brigid

ave you ever heard of St Brigid of Kildare? Of all our wonder women, Brigid of Kildare is by far the star! Brigid is so important that from February 2023, St Brigid's Day is a yearly national holiday in the Republic of Ireland. It is on the Monday closest to 1st February or, if on a Friday, it is that Friday.

Bountiful Brigid is one of Ireland's three patron saints. The other two patron saints are St Patrick and St Columba (or Colmcille in Irish). Brigid is known not just throughout Ireland but the world. She lavishly loved and served everyone, especially the poor, the destitute, prisoners, the sick, the elderly, and even animals of all kinds. There are so many wonderful stories about her that they would fill lots and lots of books! And so, our story here on Brigid is much longer than those for the other wonder women, as befits our female patron saint. It was said that an angel would need to appear to relate all her miracles and marvels as there were so many of them. Some people have also written that she performed more miracles than any other saint. It is no wonder that she became known as 'Mary of the Gael'.

From the start, it was clear that Brigid was especially holy and set apart from pagan things for God's purposes. Her father was called Dubhthach, and he was a pagan chieftain of Leinster. Her mother was a Christian, called Broicseach. Sadly, however, she was a slave owned by Dubhthach. It is hard to understand how her slavery came about, but there is one story that it happened as she was kidnapped by Irish pirates, taken to Portugal, and then somehow returned to Ireland to be sold to Dubhthach! Whatever happened, since her mother was a slave, Brigid was born as a slave too. What's more, Brigid had been born out of wedlock, so she really did have a low status at the start of her life. But from birth, Brigid showed her pagan father than she was special – though there are so many amazing occurrences surrounding her birth and whole life that I can only mention a few.

This is the first I will recall. Brigid's father and her pregnant mother, Broicseach, were travelling in a chariot one day. They passed a druid and his servants. They could hear the druid remarking that the chariot was resounding 'under a king'. His prophetic words spoke of the future greatness of Brigid. Secondly, the local druid, Maithgen, said of Brigid while her mother was pregnant with her, 'Marvellous will be the child that is in her womb… The bondmaid will bring forth a daughter conspicuous and radiant, who will shine like a sun among the stars of heaven!' Brigid was born at the foot of the Cooley mountains in Faughart, just north of Dundalk in Co. Louth. We don't know the exact year, but it was sometime between the year 436 AD and 468 AD that Brigid was born at dawn. It is said that angels hovered over her mother's cottage there and a bright light could be seen as far as Dundalk Bay. Fourthly, Brigid was born at the threshold of the door of the house. Her mother Broicseach had one foot inside the house and the other outside when Brigid's time to be born came about. This had been prophesied the day before: 'The child born tomorrow at the rising of the sun, and who is born without being inside or outside a house, that child will surpass every other child in Ireland.'

A fifth special thing that happened was that Dubhthach had a series of dreams about Brigid. Before a name had been given to his child, he had dreams of three Christian clerics baptising her. In the dream, one of the clerics told him, 'Let Brigit be your name for the girl.' Now, when Brigid was born in the fifth century, there were still many pagan people who followed the religion of the druids. Brigid was the name of a very famous Irish goddess of three sisters (each with the same name). The three Brigid goddesses were Brigid the poetess, Brigid the healer, and Brigid the smith. Dubhthach wondered to himself, 'Why on earth does my daughter deserve such an important name?' But, puffed up with pride, the pagan chieftain agreed. It was a sign of important things to come.

Now, there were seven medieval 'lives' of St Brigid, and there are some small differences in the story about where Brigid lived in her childhood. However, it would seem that Dubhthach's proper wife was jealous of Brigid's mum and insisted that Broicseach be sold. First, she was sold to a poet, then to a druid. She was sent far away, right over to the west of Ireland in the province of Connacht. However, for part of her childhood, Brigid was allowed to live with her mum and the druid, and for part of it at least she lived with her father Dubhthach in Co. Louth.

So even though Brigid was a chieftain's daughter, she was raised in part by a pagan druid, with many chores to do on his farm. She worked extremely hard, giving honour to God through this daily work. She herded sheep, pigs and cattle, and grew to love animals. However, it is the cow especially beside which Brigid is shown in religious art. To start, let me tell you the story of Brigid's red-eared cow, Bó Chluasach Dearg Bhríde. Brigid was so holy that she would vomit when the druid tried to feed her! You see, he with his pagan beliefs was impure. But God did not forget her. He sent a white cow with red ears to sustain her with its milk instead. It is significant that in old Irish folklore, white cows were sacred (so this would have been another sign that Brigid was special). Then, of course there is the story of the butter. Brigid once gave away her mother and the druid's entire supply of butter to someone in need. She then prayed for God to re-plenish the supply, and butter miraculously appeared!

When she was little, it is written that angels played with her. She built a little stone altar one day and an angel appeared to help her finish building it! And what became of the druid's beliefs? That druid became a Christian from all the mirac-ulous things Brigid did. And as a result, at some point Brigid's mum received her freedom from slavery.

When she was older, it came time for Brigid to live at her father's home. Her foster-mother wasn't pleased with that, but she had no choice, and over time Brig-id, of course, performed miracles involving her. Some say she was perhaps ten years old when she moved back to her father's home. And, of course, Brigid got up to mischief giving away copious amounts of food and other items to show God's love. Yet, when they were counted, often the things Brigid had given away were miracu-lously returned, as if they had been replaced by God. From childhood, the miracles associated with Brigid showed God's love for animals.

Once, her father had a guest and he asked Brigid to boil five pieces of bacon. Now, it happened to be that two very miserable, sad-looking hounds came into the kitchen. Those two hounds looked adoringly at the rashers, as they were extremely hungry. The bacon's smell was simply irresistible to them! Brigid had always loved animals and so she couldn't stop herself giving two pieces to the dogs. When her fa-ther asked about the bacon, she said for him to count them. She thought to herself, 'I'm really trusting God to do a miracle here!' Low and behold, all five pieces were there. Now, the guest who had appeared to be asleep while all this was happening had actually seen everything! He told her father everything, and in the end no one ate the meat. They decided to give it to the poor, as they felt that they weren't worthy of it. Yes, even her pagan father felt that way. God, you see, was working on him! Another time, Brigid was in the forest and came across a wild boar. She tamed it easily and it joined her father's livestock, so he was pleased at that miracle too.

Another day, Brigid was outside in the fields looking after her father's pigs. But perhaps something scared them because the herd separated and started to run all over the place. Two thieves appeared and took the opportunity to steal two of them! But at that second, her father Dubhthach appeared. The thieves dropped his pigs and ran. For some reason, Dubhthach wanted to test Brigid. He hid the two pigs and asked her to count the herd to check that they were all present. When Brigid counted them, they were all there. Dubhthach left scratching his head that day, surprised yet again. Strange things sure did happen around his daughter Brigid!

It must have been because of all the miracles that Brigid was actually allowed to meet the great St Patrick. Patrick was an old man at the time and Brigid, even though she was only a young girl, was known for her gifts of prophecy and miracles. At a certain meeting one day, she nodded off as it were, as if she was going to sleep. Only, it was a vision that she was having, not a nap. Patrick knew to ask Brigid about it and she told him all about it. It was about the present and future state of the Church, she said, which was another indication of Brigid's important role to the whole Church throughout Ireland (and beyond).

Meanwhile however, back at home, Brigid's charitable nature in donating all her father's possessions to the needy was making him mad beyond words. He was so angry with her one day that he took her in his chariot to the

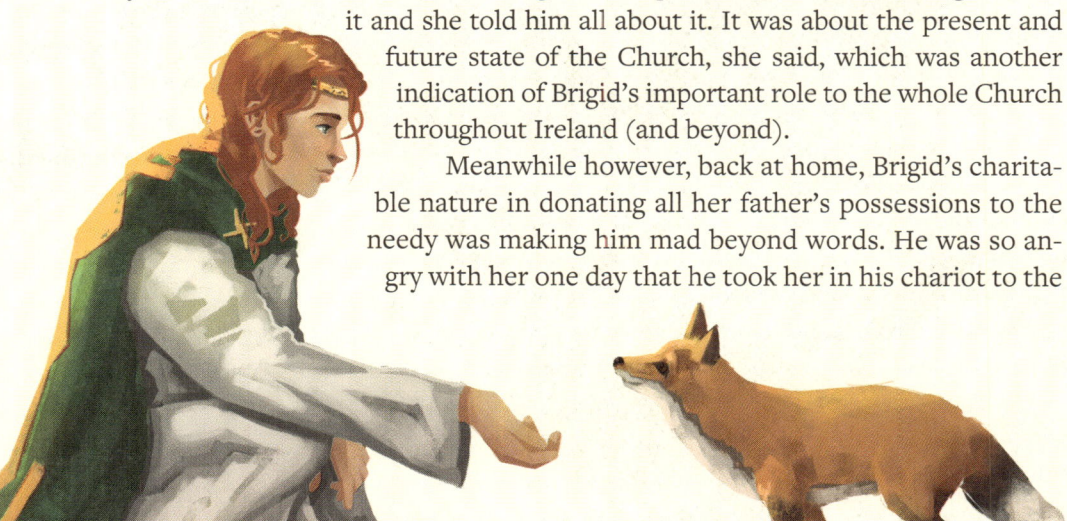

King of Leinster, hoping to sell her! He wanted to get rid of her! It's shocking to believe, but while her father was speaking to the King, Brigid actually gave away her father's jewelled sword to a beggar. She told him he should sell it and feed his family with it. Back then in ancient Ireland, a sword was a crucially important object. What would her father do the next time he had a battle to fight? However, Brigid stood up for herself and explained that serving God's kingdom by fighting poverty was more important than fighting battles in man's kingdom. The King of Leinster acknowledged Brigid's holiness and gave Dubhthach another sword to replace the one that Brigid had given away. Better still, he even convinced Dubhthach to give Brigid her freedom.

We come now to that part in the story when Brigid was of age and her father presented her with potential suitors who he had chosen for her to marry. It is said that he presented her with two suitors, one a king and the other a poet. One rich in money, the other also of very high status in early Ireland. The poet was none other than Dubthach maccu Lugair. He became the top poet in Ireland, chief Olam. He was also an expert lawyer in old Irish law, the Brehon laws. But Brigid put her foot down and told him she couldn't accept his proposal. However, she put her gift of prophecy to good use and told him, 'Go to the woods behind your house where I know for sure that you would find a beautiful maiden to marry! The maiden's parents will be very pleased to allow you to marry her'. So, Dubthach the poet-lawyer followed Brigid's instructions, and everything happened as she had said. Dubthach at some point even became a Christian; Brigid probably had a hand in that too!

However, there is another version of the story and perhaps this is about the king who came to woo her. What comes next is shocking! Brigid thought to God that she didn't care about how she looked. She prayed that God would make her ugly! All the better for focusing on her true destiny, a bride of Christ; spending her time serving God alone. Well, the next morning, she awoke to discover her entire face swollen like a balloon. There is also a story that Brigid had brothers and that, at this, they were annoyed at the loss of a bride price (money paid by the groom to the bride's family). While Brigid was outside carrying some firewood past a group of poor people, some began to laugh at her. A man named Bacene (some say he was her brother) said to her, 'The beautiful eye which is in your head will be betrothed to a man, though you like it or not.' Brigid's response was to push her finger into her eye. She said, 'Here is that beautiful eye for you. I deem it unlikely that anyone will ask you for a blind girl!' Her brothers tried to help her and wash away the blood from her wound, but there was no water to be found. Brigid said to them, 'Put my staff about this sod (of earth) in front of you.' After they did, a stream came out from the ground. Then Brigid said to Bacene, 'Soon your two eyes will burst in your head.' And it all happened as she said. Later, however, Brigid's eye was miraculously replaced! Once both suitors withdrew, Brigid got her good looks back.

And so, bountiful Brigid became a nun. And as if that wasn't enough, the story continues that either St Mac Caille of Croghan Hill, Co. Offaly or St Mel of Ardagh made her a bishop. St Mel was a nephew of St Patrick. In some versions of the story, Brigid being made a bishop was sort of an accident. Some say the wrong prayers were said. When asked about it, St Mel replied that the Holy Spirit had taken the matter out of his hands and made him drunk with the Holy Spirit! When Brigid was being ordained a bishop, a brilliant flame ascended from her head. (Fire is a symbol of the Holy Spirit). And so Brigid and every Abbess successor at Kildare were bishops, until 1152 AD in the twelfth century.

Soon after, we come to one of the best-known stories about Brigid: the wonderful tale of Brigid's expanding cloak. Brigid was a pioneer; brilliant at starting churches in areas where there were none yet. Now, she knew the King of Leinster, the one who had so kindly persuaded her father to give her freedom from slavery. So, she asked him for some land for a monastery. The location she chose was ideal; it was near a lake (so they would have plenty of water), in a forest (so they would have lots of firewood), and near a fertile plain (so they could grow plenty of crops). But the King refused her request. Not being put off, Brigid prayed that his heart would be softened. After, she asked him again, and this time she added, 'Give me as much land as my cloak will cover!' The King looked at her small cloak and laughed, but he granted her wish. He obviously thought Brigid was making a joke. Brigid must have been taken over by prophetic inspiration! She had a brilliant idea. She got four of her nuns to take a corner each and walk in opposite directions. Slowly, then running with joy, the four women went off in the compass directions. North, south, east, west! It wasn't long until Brigid's four helpers couldn't see each other! The cloak grew and grew, spreading across acres and acres of land. Brigid now had plenty of land for her monastery. It is written that the King and his household were in a mixture of bamboozlement and amazement. But he hadn't been tricked. Even though he was dismayed, he realised that Brigid was truly blessed by God. The King became a patron of Brigid's monastery, assisting her with money, food and gifts to give to the poor. Later, he even became a Christian.

The place in the forest where Brigid started her monastery was by an oak tree. Traditionally, the oak was the sacred tree of the druids. It is the longest-living native deciduous tree of Ireland, so it would have had special significance that Brigid chose that site. Even today, the Irish oak (sessile oak) is the national tree of Ireland. The place became known as Kildare (Cill Dara), 'church of the oak'. Here, Bishop Brigid started a dual monastery for men and women; monks and nuns. The church building was, of course, built out of oak. At first, Brigid started out with seven nuns, but it wasn't long before the numbers steadily grew. Soon she had so many to care for that she asked the monk, St Conleth, to assist her as Bishop, with her in the role of Abbess Bishop. In time, it is said that Brigid ended up being in charge of more than 10,000 nuns!

Now, a perpetual flame burned in Kildare in pre-Christian times. Scholars suggest that priestesses used to gather on the hill there to tend this ritual fire, while invoking the goddesses called Brigid to protect their herds and provide a fruitful harvest. Brigid, making a point that God would protect and provide, continued that custom. The fire represented the Holy Spirit and the new light of Christianity. In Brigid's time, the number of her nuns who tended the flame was 19. On the twentieth day, Brigid tended it herself. The twelfth- and thirteenth-century Gerald of Wales wrote a guide to Ireland, in which he described how it never produced any ash and was surrounded by a hedge, which no man was allowed to enter! Only women were allowed to tend to the fire and blow on it. Gerald told a story about how an archer tried to defy this by leaping over the hedge and blowing on the fire. The archer began to lose his senses and blew into everyone's faces. Then, taken over by thirst, he begged his friends to take him to some nearby water, where he drank so much that he burst. Yes, it is said that he burst! The sacred flame survived for hundreds of years. Possibly up to the suppression of the monasteries in the sixteenth century. In 1993, the flame was re-lit in the Market Square of Kildare, by the then congregational leader of the Brigidine Sisters (named after Brigid). The flame comes out of a lovely sculpture, in the shape of an acorn with oak leaves.

But Brigid didn't just stay home all day tending a sacred fire. No, she often left Kildare to chariot throughout the whole of Ireland to supervise the building of other monasteries. Her trusty chariot driver was called Natfroich. The rumble of chariot wheels was no doubt a welcome sound to the poor and destitute. She took seriously Jesus's command in the Bible to 'love your neighbour as yourself' (Matthew 22:39, Mark 12:31, Luke 10:27), and she did so with abundance. We also know that of all the eight 'beatitudes' in Jesus' famous Sermon on the Mount, Brigid focused on showing mercy to people.

Not only would people have welcomed the sound of Brigid's chariot, they would have been familiar with the *moo* of her white cow. Brigid and her famous white cow wandered the breadth of Ireland. Across the island she went, telling and showing people the good news of Jesus. Her marvellous white cow supplied huge amounts of milk to everyone who needed it.

Once, there was a cow who had been milked dry. But Brigid touched and blessed her, then gave that cow then to some starving poor people, and when they milked her, the cow, instead of having no milk, provided ten times as much milk as one would expect any ordinary cow to provide!

Once Brigid's monastery ran out of milk for their own needs. A large number of bishops had arrived, so Brigid asked Bláth, the nun who was their cook, to provide a feast for them. Bláth said, 'I'm sorry. We don't have any food for these fine gentlemen.' Brigid prayed and an angel appeared who said, 'Brigid, milk your cows.' Brigid said, 'The cows have been milked twice already today. I don't think they have any more milk.' But the angel told her again to milk the cows, so Brigid got her wooden bucket and went to the shed to milk the cows herself. She wanted to see for herself what would happen... milk filled every single pail that she had. It is said that it would have filled all the pails in Leinster. The milk kept on coming and it overflowed those buckets until it formed a lake! Even today that lake is known as the Lake of Milk or Lake of the New Milk ('Loch Leamnachta' in Irish).

In another story, when Brigid had guests but no food, it is written that she changed nettles into butter and tree bark into 'the richest and most delicious bacon'. Can you imagine it? Would you like to taste nettles and tree bark, turned into food?

Another day, while she was on one of her chariot trips, Brigid came across a group of poor people who were suffering because of a drought (a lack of rain). Knowing that a miracle was needed, she told them to dig at a certain spot in the ground. Low and behold, a new well with fresh water was discovered! But that wasn't enough for Bountiful Brigid; she generously handed over her horses to help them. Now, a prince just happened to come through at that same time, looking for water for his horse. He used the new well and heard the whole story. Overcome with a smaller kindness himself (as he was rich), he gave Brigid two of his own horses as thanks. The prince's horses were unbroken and wild, but Brigid, accustomed to caring for animals, took hold of them and they were as untroubled and docile as could be.

Another day, Brigid visited the King of Leinster's castle. Brigid admired the harps hung around the great hall. She asked, 'Who plays the harp?' But the King was away and all his harpers too. So the King's sons told her that no one there was able to play. But Brigid loved music, so she reached over to the sons' fingers and blessed them. They took down the harps and played. The harp music was the most beautiful that had ever been heard in that hall! When the King returned, he was enchanted and said, 'You may have anything that is in my power to give.' Without a hesitation, Brigid asked for all the prisoners to be released. He wasn't expecting that!

Not only did Brigid care for the poor and prisoners, but also the sick (often also poor as a result). One day, Brigid had a headache, but she believed not just in praying for things but also using doctors, so off she set to see a doctor. When she was away, she stayed at the house of a Leinster couple who had two mute daughters (they couldn't speak). The daughters were travelling with Brigid when Brigid's horse got spooked by something. Brigid actually fell off her chariot and grazed her head on a stone. There was a little bit of blood and a touch of it healed the two girls of their muteness.

In another story, there was a woman who had received a beautiful and expensive silver brooch from a nobleman. For some reason, she had thrown it into the sea. The nobleman charged her with stealing, even though it had been given to her as a gift. He then planned to make her his slave if a judge ruled in his favour. The woman fled to Brigid and her monastery to seek refuge. Brigid heard the whole story. She hated slavery, knowing from personal experience what it was like. It was an awful, evil of society in early Ireland. So again, Brigid prayed about the situation. And very soon one of her fishermen hauled in a fish and what should be in its stomach when he cut it open? The brooch! The fish had swallowed it. And what became of the nobleman? He freed the woman, confessed his sin and bowed to Brigid.

Brigid is also famous for caring for the lonely. She encouraged people to be friends. In one well-known saying, she said, 'A person without a soul friend ('anam cara' in Irish) is like a body without a head.'

37

Brigid didn't just provide in large quantities, she taught people to do the same. Some of those in her monastery got a bit grumpy when they went without, so others could be provided for. Often Brigid taught them lessons about it. One day she was out and about when a woman gave her a gift of apples and sloes (the fruit from the blackthorn). Later, she entered a house of lepers who begged her for the apples. They couldn't go out to work, so they had nothing. Brigid gladly gave them the apples. But the woman who gave Brigid the fruit heard about it and was very angry. She said she had given them to Brigid, not lepers! Brigid was very annoyed and wanted to teach her a lesson, so she cursed the woman's trees so they couldn't bear fruit anymore. On the other hand, another woman gave Brigid the same gift and, again, Brigid gave them to begging lepers. This woman had the opposite attitude. She asked that she and her garden be blessed. So Brigid pointed at a particular tree in her garden and said it would have twice as much fruit, which it did.

Another group that Brigid cared for were the elderly. One of her most famous symbols is her cross. This is the story of how it came to be. One day, she was visiting an old chieftain who was close to death. She knew that his time to depart the Earth was close and cared about his soul. So she wondered how she could explain the good news about God to him. She picked up some of the rushes that were carpeting his floor. And, as she weaved, she prayed for inspiration and explained the story about the life and death of Jesus. The old chieftan was curious about the shape that she was weaving and Brigid looked down to see that she had made a cross. He was so touched that he asked to be baptised before he died. And so Brigid's distinctive cross is woven throughout Ireland, and many other parts of the world, in memory of Brigid and her message about Jesus.

According to tradition, a new cross is woven on each St Brigid's Eve on 31st January. The old one is burned to protect the house from fire. Some believe that keeping a cross in the rafters preserves the house from fire and disease. In Brigid's time, most of the houses had straw, thatch and wood for roofs. The cross is also placed under the barn eaves or in the cow byre to protect the animals. Its often first sprinkled in holy water. There are actually many different shapes to St Brigid's crosses. You can see some of them at the National Museum of Ireland – Country Life in Castlebar, Co. Mayo. The four-legged cross was the symbol of RTÉ until 1995 and is still the symbol of the Nursing and Midwifery Board of Ireland.

Brigid also taught everyone about heaven. She had a vision of heaven as a great lake of beer and everyone experiencing great hospitality there! God's family were drinking the beer through all eternity. In those days, you see, drinking water wasn't necessarily clean as the bacteria in it could cause illness, even death. Drinking beer (or ale) was a normal (and vital) activity. Hops were not grown in Ireland at that time, so Brigid made 'ale' rather than beer. It would have had a much lower alcoholic content than ales sold today. This was at a time when tea and coffee didn't exist in Ireland until more than 1,000 years later!

One day when Brigid had lepers as guests, she realised that she had no ale to give to them. It is written that 'with the power of her faith' she was able to turn bathwater into ale! In another story, she supplied seventeen churches with enough ale to last for eleven days over Easter, despite having only one barrel. Not only did she turn water into ale, she could turn milk into ale!

There is a poem (written later, possibly in the tenth century, but attributed to St Brigid) about her vision of a lake of beer in heaven. There are also other versions of it.

I'd like to give a lake of beer to God.
I'd love the heavenly
Host to be tippling there
For all eternity.

I'd love the men of Heaven to live with me,
To dance and sing.
If they wanted, I'd put at their disposal
Vats of suffering.

White cups of love I'd give them
With a heart and a half;
Sweet pitchers of mercy I'd offer
To every man.

I'd make Heaven a cheerful spot
Because the happy heart is true.
I'd make the men contented for their own sake.
I'd like Jesus to love me too.

I'd like the people of heaven to gather
From all the parishes around.
I'd give a special welcome to the women,
The three Marys of great renown.

I'd sit with the men, the women and God
There by the lake of beer.
We'd be drinking good health forever
And every drop would be a prayer.

Not only did Brigid care for the prisoners, the poor, sick and elderly, she also founded a school of art. She appointed St Conleth in charge of it. They made wonderfully beautiful items in the fields of illuminated manuscripts and metalwork. Brigid's Kildare scriptorium made the Book of Kildare, which drew huge praise from the twelfth- and thirteenth-century Gerald of Wales. It was so lovely it was said to be more beautiful than even the *Book of Kells*. But sadly, it disappeared during the Protestant Reformation. Gerald of Wales said nothing he ever saw was at all comparable to the book. Every page was gorgeously illuminated, interlaced and nothing had such harmony of colours. He said, 'all this is the work of angelic, and not human skill!'

As well as famously travelling Ireland with her white cow, Brigid was known as a shepherdess. She loved being out in the fields of Kildare with her sheep and lambs. She worked hard every day. She had known from when she was a young girl what it was like to be a farmer, despite being a chieftain's daughter.

Did you know that there is a flower associated with St Brigid? Dandelions are known in Irish as 'Bearnán Bríde' ('the indented one of Brigid'). Have you ever picked dandelions? If you have, you will know that there is a white milky-looking sap that comes out from the stem. And so it is said that just as the dandelion's milky sap feeds young lambs, so Brigid the shepherdess protected her sheep.

It's already been mentioned in our story that Brigid had a wonderful way with animals, both domestic and wild. This next story is about a fox ('sionnach', or 'madra rua' in Irish, meaning 'red dog'). One day, a friend of the monastery came to Brigid with a terrible tale. A friend had accidentally killed a fox in the woods. It turned out that the fox belonged to the King of Leinster. It had been his pet fox, not a wild one! So the King's guard had arrested the man. His distraught wife and children begged clemency for the man. It was a genuine mistake after all. But the King was distressed himself and not feeling too forgiving. He wanted vengeance! Brigid was asked to intervene. She valued the life of animals but thought the king was being unjust. It was silly that a human's life should be demanded in exchange for the life of a fox. She set out to plead the case of the woodsman. As she went along, she took a path through the woods. Praying as she went and thinking over what she was going to say, who should she see but a little fox cub! She called to it and the young fox trotted over to her. Brigid had an idea and the little fox let her carry it to the King's castle. When Brigid got there, the King paid no heed to Brigid's pleas; he wanted the death penalty for the woodsman. Then Brigid got out the little fox. She asked the fox to do some trick and, of course, the little fox understood her. For that was just the way Brigid had with animals, a fifth to sixth-century Dr. Dolittle! The hard heart of the King was soon melted. The most amazing thing was that this little fox could do all the tricks of the King's own pet fox. So the King relented and granted a pardon to his prisoner. Brigid left the little fox with the King, who loved it dearly. Though, the day came when the King left on business, and the little fox cunningly saw its chance to escape back to its home in the woods. The King's men sent out search parties for it, but it was never seen again.

Another wonderful story that shows Brigid's power over animals is the story of 'St Brendan and the sea monsters'. While on one of his ocean voyages, St Brendan came across two sea monsters caught up in a terrible battle. The one that was being pursued said in a human voice to the other, 'I commend myself to the protection of St Patrick, the Chief-Bishop of the Irish!' The other monster said, 'his protection will now avail you nothing!' The losing monster cried out, 'I commend myself to the protection of St Brendan, here present,' and his pursuer replied, 'neither will *his* protection save you now!' At last, in exasperation the poor sea monster, possibly about to be gobbled up by the other, said, 'I commend myself to the protection of the most holy virgin, Brigid!' Immediately, that did the trick. The pursuing sea monster left straight away! Then St Brendan composed a hymn in praise of St Brigid, and the next time he met her asked her why even such animals respected her. Her secret was that, never for even a minute, did she not think about God.

Another day, a wild boar came crashing through the fields at Kildare. But just as she had done in her childhood with another wild boar, Brigid tamed it and it joined her herd of domestic pigs. Not one wild bone was left in its body! Another day, Brigid was taking some nicely fatted pigs quite a distance from the plain of the River Barrow to Dunshaughlin, Co. Meath. It was a three- or four-day journey. What on earth should appear from the forest, but wild wolves! Instead of helping themselves to a lunch of piggy pork and bacon though, the wolves helped Brigid escort the pigs, all the way to Co. Meath.

On yet another day, Brigid was out walking near a pond or lake. Ducks were enjoying their swim in the water and flying about in the air. Brigid loved animals so much that she called them over to herself. What do you think should happen? These completely wild ducks came over to her and flew into Brigid's outstretched arms! She held them and stroked their feathers before she let fly off again.

As well as travelling all over Ireland, it is said that Brigid went to Glastonbury in England. She also went to Scotland and started a whole string of monasteries there too. She was sailing across in her currach near the shore of South Uist in the Outer Hebrides, when she heard, *bi glic!*, *bi glic!*, *bi glic!*, *bi glic!* Brigid knew that it was from Gaelic and meant, 'be wise, be careful, take care.' It was coming from the birds! They were oystercatchers ('Roilleach' in Irish). What a wonderful welcome! Everywhere around her were these black and white birds with their long, orange-red bills and reddish-pink legs. When the local people saw her getting out of her currach, she had a friendly oystercatcher on each of her wrists. Soon, locals were calling the oystercatchers 'gille Bride' ('servant of Bride') and 'bridein ('bird of Bride'). Bride is Brigid's name shortened, you see.

And there are some even more wonderful legends about how God used the oystercatchers in Brigid's life. One day, some evil men were chasing after Brigid, trying to kill her! Brigid, quite unlike herself, collapsed on the sandy beach by the sea and prayed for God's help. God sent the oystercatchers, who quickly covered her whole body with seaweed. When the evil men arrived, they couldn't see a trace of her! Another day, three very young children were out at sea all alone. A storm blew up and they were adrift, too young to sail back to shore. Two oystercatchers saw them and flew to Brigid to get help. Brigid got in her currach and the oyster-catchers guided her to the infants. God had used Brigid and the oystercatchers to save the day again! Yet another day while Brigid was on her way to Barra in the Outer Hebrides, Brigid this time found herself caught in a storm. Her little currach rocked back and forth, buffeted by winds from every direction, so that it made no progress towards her destination. Who should appear, but her oystercatchers! They flapped the wind into her sail so the currach moved in the right direction and soon she was ashore at Barra.

If you ever see an oystercatcher flying, you will notice that it is white underneath, in the shape of a cross. The legend is that Brigid gave it this shape in memory of Christ's cross. And it is white, in memory of her own white cloak that she is said to have sometimes worn.

In her later years, Brigid's powers became even greater. She went into battle before the King of Leinster, with fire blazing from her head. Once after a rainy day of taking care of her sheep, she hung her damp cloak on a sunbeam of light to dry, commanding the sunbeam to remain all night. The sunbeam did indeed stay all night. She multiplied food and drink, exorcised demons with a simple sign of the cross and could calm storms! It is written that, 'she stilled the rain and wind'. One harvest day, when they were bringing in the crops, there was torrential rain all around them. But at Brigid's monastery, it was dry all day from sunrise to sunset. Everywhere else surrounding them, it had rained so hard that pools of water formed on the ground.

Brigid also walked on water. Once, she and her nuns were trying to cross the River Shannon, but the ferryman was charging an extravagant fee. So Brigid's nuns asked her to make the sign of the cross so they could walk over. In they got into the water. There were strong men and soldiers there at the time and they couldn't cross, but when Brigid and her nuns went in, the water didn't come up beyond their knees!

When Brigid was an old lady, she had a revelation four years before her death that the time for her departure was approaching. She nominated her favourite nun, Dar Lugdach, to succeed her as Abbess at Kildare for one year after she died. Dar Lugdach then died too, after exactly a year. There are so many dates suggested for the year of Brigid's death that we can't be sure exactly what year she died. It would have been sometime between 504 AD and 548 AD. But we do know that she was an older lady when she died, between 71 and 87 years old according to Dr. Noel Kissane. She had lived a long and wonderful life.

After her death, Brigid's following continued to grow even more, as manuscripts about her were translated into French, English and German. Countless churches were named after her. Initially, she was buried at Kildare, but then, about the year 878 because of Viking raids, her relics were moved. In 1185, the Anglo-Norman knight, John de Courcy, had her remains reburied in Down Cathedral, Downpatrick, along with those of St Patrick and St Columba.

The three goddesses called Brigid were especially remembered on 1st February. 1st February was called Imbolc/Imbolg, an old pagan agricultural festival. Some say Brigid died on 1st February. Others believe that 1st February was chosen as Brigid's feast day to show that she fulfilled and replaced their role as a patron of the arts, healing and metalworking. All three of these things were done at Kildare. Whatever you believe, the stories are certainly intertwined!

Of all our wonder women, Brigid is the star,
Famous in my lands, both near and afar.
From north to south, east to west, she's Ireland's patron saint,
Bountiful in showing love, and that's not something quaint!

She wandered Ireland with her cow, all white,
Feeding poor, healing ill, she showed God's might.
With daily giveaways of her cows' dairy,
Butter and milk made the people merry!

She had a vision of heaven as a lake of beer,
So with ale and good cheer, she abolished fear.
She loved her neighbour as herself,
She gave away her convent's wealth.

The yellow dandelions are her flower,
Their milky sap reminds of God's power.
You know spring is here when they appear,
Food for lambs, which she held dear.

Wild boar, ducks, horses, fox she'd tame,
Wolves, fish, sea monsters, oystercatchers, the same!
Famous for her cloak which grew and grew,
And her cross of rushes which you can make too!

44

One of the goddess sisters called Brigid was in charge of poetry.
Write your own poem about St Brigid of Kildare. It could be a general
poem about her life or about your favourite part of her story.

DID YOU KNOW?

- **Feast day:** 1st February (Lá Fhéile Bríde)

- **Other names:** Brigit, Bridget, Brighid, Brid, Bride, Bríga, Brigitte, Bridie, Bree, Brídín, Biddy, Breeda. These are just some of them!

- In 1283, during the Crusades, three Irish knights brought St Brigid's skull to Portugal. It was placed in a church at Lumiar near Lisbon. The feast day for moving the relic is 25th January.

- In the National Museum of Ireland in Dublin, there is a shrine of St Brigid's shoe. Assistant Keeper of Irish Antiquities, Ms. Sharon Weadick, let me know that it is made of gilt copper alloy. It has beautiful decorations all over it.

- Part of St Brigid's cloak is said to be in St Salvator's Cathedral in Bruges, Belgium. The story is that it was brought there by King Harold of England's sister after the Norman invasion. It is a small square of red woollen cloth with curly tufts, though faded to brown now.

- There are a huge number of places throughout the world named after St Brigid. There is even a St Brigid Island in Antarctica!

- A legend says Brigid is responsible for the Irish tradition of women being allowed to propose to men in leap years on 29th February.

- The colour associated with Brigid is white, worn by Kildare sports teams. The Kildare Gaelic football team are known as 'the Lily-Whites'.

- Dr. Noel Kissane wrote that there are 116 holy wells dedicated to St Brigid. Possibly because Brigid is said to have toured the whole of Ireland...

- There are stories that Brigid was transported to Bethlehem to help the Virgin Mary when she was giving birth to baby Jesus!

45

Buono Brigid

In Italian, 'buono' means 'kind', 'good', and even 'angelic', which gives a tiny hint at the story to come. Brigid, named after her famous namesake from Kildare in Ireland, had all those qualities; she was good and kind. And as you'll soon read, angels and the country of Italy were involved. To differentiate her from Brigid of Kildare, Buono Brigid is usually called Brigid the Younger.

We don't know where in Ireland Brigid was born, but we know Áed mac Néill (d. 819) was High King at the time. We also know Brigid's parents were aristocratic. That means they were richer than most people. As was more common with noble families they were able to send off their son, Brigid's older brother Andrew, to be a missionary. So off he set with his friend Donatus to tell people about Jesus. Donatus had been teaching both Brigid and Andrew about God and the Bible, and he was a great friend to them. Brigid was very sad to see her brother Andrew head off, but she knew it was a sacrifice the family had to make.

After visiting Rome to receive the Pope's blessing, Donatus and Andrew ended up in a town further north. That town was called Fiesole and it was in the region of Tuscany. This is in the modern-day country of Italy. They were just walking into Fiesole when Donatus turned to Andrew, wondering out loud, 'Where do you think everyone is, Andrew?' Through the streets they walked, until they approached a church and suddenly heard a *Ding, ding, ding dong...ding, dong, ding dong...ding, ding!* It was loud peeling of bells from inside. Donatus and Andrew peaked through the church doors and saw that all the people were inside the church. It was also completely lit up by what seemed to be a supernatural light! Stunned faces stared at them both. Donatus and Andrew thought, 'why are they looking at us so surprised?'

Well, the people told them why they looked surprised. It turned out that not long ago their previous bishop of the church had met a horrid end. The lords of

46

that area, who owned the land, had drowned their poor bishop! So, their church (now called the Cathedral of Saint Romulus) had no bishop. 'We decided to all meet and pray together, as we thought only God could help us,' they explained to Donatus and Andrew. 'We were asking God for a sign from heaven about what we should do, as no one here that we know of wants the job of being bishop, as we are all too scared of the wicked lords. Then a few minutes ago, our church bells suddenly began to ring when no human was ringing them! Then, as we gasped in wonder at that, the candles throughout our church building all went out but were replaced by a supernatural glow. We heard a voice say, 'Receive the stranger who approaches, Donatus of Scotia, and take him for your shepherd!' ('Scotia' back then meant someone from Ireland). 'Then,' the people continued, 'you both opened the church doors!' Well, the people of Fiesole all took that as a sign that their prayers had been heard. And so that is how Donatus ended up becoming the bishop of Fiesole and Andrew the archdeacon. Donatus and Andrew served in Fiesole for many years – Donatus was bishop there for forty-seven years (829–876 AD). During that time it wasn't all smooth sailing, as they say. The Normans attacked Fiesole and yet again, for it wasn't the first time, Fiesole's church building was damaged by invaders. Donatus was not only very wise, he was a friend and adviser of important and powerful people; for example, Emperors Louis the Pious and Lothair I. However, we won't tell Donatus and Andrew's whole story here, for this is Andrew's sister's story... Brigid's story.

As those years stretched out, far away from Ireland in Italy, Andrew often talked about his sister Brigid to the people of Fiesole. The people of Fiesole in Italy knew so many things about Brigid – about how she was kind and good. They often wished that they could meet her, as if Donatus and Andrew were such wonderful leaders, surely Brigid must be too. Now, in 377 AD, Brigid's brother Andrew took very ill. A considerable number of years had passed since Brigid and Andrew had seen each other. Andrew, still very close in heart to his beloved sister, was able to pick up ink and write a letter to Brigid. One morning, Brigid heard a horse clip-clopping up to her home. She had just been having her lunch of some small fish and a salad. The messenger on the horse had brought her Andrew's letter. When she read the news that Andrew was close to death, Brigid was overcome with grief. She prayed and prayed. Sobbing with tears, she went out into her garden, wandering down to the bottom of it by the little orchard full of apple trees. There she sat

47

on her favourite bench and prayed between her sobs. Normally this was the place that made her the happiest, with its beautiful flowers and tall trees and fruit, but today, tears streamed down her face so much that her vision was blurred...and she could hardly trust what she was now seeing! Two golden angels had appeared beside her. No divine trumpets heralded their arrival; they just floated down from the sky. Happy smiles beamed from their faces.

'Brigid! Exalted one!' – this is what Brigid's name meant in Irish (and the angels were being very nice to her calling her that). 'You are needed far away in Fiesole!' Brigid had known this since she'd received the letter, but never in a million years could she have guessed what was about to happen next. Without another word, one angel lifted her head and shoulders, while the other lifted her feet! Up and up they miraculously ascended through the clouds. They flew over land and sea. They left confused *moo*ing cows far below in green Irish fields, only to be greeted by the *squawk* of astonished sea gulls ('Faoileán' in Irish) flying beside them! An inquisitive seal ('Rón' in Irish) peeped up from the deep blue sea as they passed over it.

Much, much sooner than you might expect, Brigid and the two angels were in Tuscany. She could see the beautiful city of Florence close by as she approached. Fiesole was on a mountain dotted with wealthy villas (houses) and formal gardens, just 3 miles (5 km) northeast of Florence. One of the angels, eyes bright with love and kindness, said to Brigid (to distract her from her grief), 'Dear Brigid, you will find this interesting. Many, many years in the future people will fly in machines that they have made, in the sky! One very famous artist and scientist, called Leonardo da Vinci, will try out his early flying models on these hills around Fiesole!' And do you know, it happened exactly as the angel said. Leonardo da Vinci (1452-1519 AD), lived in the fifteenth and sixteenth centuries, and indeed he carried out his flying experiments for the first time exactly where Brigid now was.

Brigid and the angels passed over the ancient ruins of the Roman theatre, baths and Etruscan walls just before they dropped to the ground. I'm sure you've heard of the Romans, but you probably haven't heard of the Etruscans. They were also an old civilisation that used to live in that area. You see, Fiesole was an extremely beautiful, ancient town.

Andrew and Brigid were both delighted to see each other after so many decades. However, Andrew was very close to passing to heaven. It gave them both great comfort to be able to share those few last minutes together at Andrew's bedside. As Brigid held

Andrew's hand, she spoke some last words to him and prayed. There was not only the comfort of that, but the whole thing made a huge impact on the people of Fiesole. The news of Christianity spread even further afield, because of Brigid's miraculous journey with the angels. After Andrew died, Brigid had a lot to think about. She pondered what the angels had said, that she was needed in Fiesole. Might God mean that she should remain in Tuscany and serve the people there?

Brigid decided to stay; but there was one problem. 'Dear God, where will I live now?' she prayed, then she meditated on what she needed and where would best suit those needs. She knew she wanted some time alone. Then she also thought back to her favourite spot in Ireland – the bottom of her garden by the apple orchard. 'Yes,' thought Brigid, 'it was a perfect spot to pray and think about God, because the flowers and trees were so beautiful...just like God.' At this, she decided to live a large part of her time up in the Northern Apennine Mountains. The Apennines' sheer magnitude and beauty made it easy to reflect on God as creator and also gave her solitude.

Brigid found a simple hermit's home in a cave in the forest. It was some distance to the northeast of Fiesole. The place where she lived was called Opacum (or Opacus), near Lobaco at the foot of the steep mountains. Her only company was the wild animals. But it was near a little river called Sieci, so she had plenty of clean drinking water. She mostly spent her time walking in the woods, gathering fruit and roots to eat, and praying. Sometimes local hunters who had caught deer or rabbits came to her cave and offered her them to cook. But Brigid always turned them down, as she wanted to eat simply. She also fasted (went without food) a lot. However, she didn't forget the angels' words and so looked after the people of Fiesole. She put into practice everything that Donatus had taught her brother and herself as a child. She healed the blind, as well as the sick and those who couldn't walk.

The people of Fiesole were well-known for being very wealthy in money – many of them were rich. They were even richer than the people of the big city of Florence, to the southwest. Brigid, knowing that God wanted her to speak to them about this, used her Bible knowledge. After all, the Bible taught that to be a Christian it is essential to look after the poor. It also taught that the love of money can be a root of all kinds of evil. This below is a Bible verse that she used to teach the people of Fiesole. Can you understand what it means?

No one can serve two masters. Either you will hate the one and love the other, or you will be devoted to the one and despise the other. You cannot serve both God and money.
– Matthew 6:24, NIV

Brigid spent some wonderful years in Tuscany. There had been a saying from the people of the nearby city of Florence that the people of Fiesole were cruel and barbaric. But Brigid learnt that that was only because of wars, rivalries and misunderstanding. Indeed, we know from years later in a very famous poetic story called 'The Divine Comedy', written by Dante between 1308-1320, that the people of Florence referred to those in Fiesole as 'the beasts of Fiesole' (Inferno XV:73). Brigid never experienced any beastly behaviour while she was there.

When Brigid died, the people buried her and built a church dedicated to her memory. This was called Santa Brigida. Pilgrimages were made to her shrine there long after her death. Even today, people travel to Santa Brigida to visit the church, as well as the cave and statue of her that is there. She might not be as well-known as Brigid of Kildare, but the people of Fiesole and Ireland have not forgotten her!

Which part of Brigid the Younger's Story did you like the best?

51

TASK:

Can you find Italy on a map of Europe? Can you see the route the angels and Brigid might have taken? What modern-day countries are between Ireland and Italy?

DID YOU KNOW?

❋ **Feast days:** 1st February (in Italy) & 20th August (not celebrated).

❋ Some people don't believe that Brigid was a real person! They think that she was mixed up with Brigid of Kildare. This is partly because they share the same Feast Day in Italy and also because Brigid of Kildare is also supposed to have been carried by angels to see St Donatus when he was dying.

❋ There is a beautiful painting by the Scottish artist, John Duncan, of St Brigid of Kildare being carried by angels. I love the sea gulls flying beside them. There is also an inquisitive seal peeping up from the sea as they pass over. The painting might look something similar to the angels carrying Brigid of Fiesole to Tuscany. It was an inspiration for part of my story!

Brónach & her Bell

L ong ago, a little girl grew up near Slemish Mountain (Sliabh Mis), in pagan Co. Antrim in Ulster. It was in the northeast of Ireland. That girl was called Brónach. Her name, rather unusually, meant 'sorrowful'. It wasn't a common name and Brónach, even from a tender age, was determined not to let it decide her fate in life! She didn't want to be sad and sorrowful. Another thing to know about Brónach was that she had strange dreams at night, and visions, even while awake. She had a particular series of repeated dreams from when she was young. Dreams could be powerful things, and were always to be taken heed of. In her dreams, Brónach fought one of the most powerful Irish gods (the Tuatha Dé Danann). That god was called Manannán mac Lir ('son of the sea'). He was, as the druids taught, god of the sea. Now, as a girl, Brónach lived nowhere particularly near the sea, so she pondered those dreams long and hard. What could they mean? Manannán was known as a powerful warrior and King of the Other-world in Irish mythology. In pagan Ireland, for those who followed druid beliefs, he was a god to fear on the seas, as your life was in his hands. He rode across the waves with his chariot, led by his horse Enbarr, who could cross both land and sea, swifter than the wind!

Brónach's father was an important man. His name was Míliuc mac Buan, better known as Milchú. He was a chief of the Dál mBuain, mainly in Co. Antrim (but with parts in Co. Down), in Ulster. What is key to our story is that Brónach's father, Milchú, was the man who kept the great St Patrick in slavery as a boy at Slemish Mountain, Co. Antrim. Years later, after Patrick escaped from slavery, he returned to Ireland. Tradition has it that Brónach and her brothers, Gall and Guasacht, along with her two sisters (both called Éimhear) all heard the gospel and became Christians at that time when they heard Patrick speak. Since he was back in Ireland, he

53

probably went to Milchú's home to convert him and his family. Brónach's life was forever changed. Indeed, her brother Gall became a priest and later a bishop in the area of Dromore, Co. Down. And her brother Guasacht was appointed the first bishop of Granard in Co. Longford by St Patrick. Her two sisters were also church leaders (perhaps at Clonbroney, Co. Longford)!

Meanwhile, Brónach had more dreams when she slept, and visions while awake. She dreamt that, like her brothers and sisters, she became a church leader and started a church. But where to locate her church? Where did God want her to go? Then she remembered her recurring childhood dreams of Manannán mac Lir, the sea God. Perhaps she should set up that church near the sea and look after sailors and fishermen? The local people all believed that Manannán mac Lir was a god, and so would decide if they lived or drowned at sea. Brónach needed to tell them the truth, which is that God from the Bible would take care of them, even at sea!

Then, Brónach had further dreams and visions of hundreds and hundreds of brent geese ('Cadhan' in Irish). These were light-bellied brent geese, to be precise, and they were flying past her. But one was at her feet. She would wake up in the mornings, her head still filled with their honking sounds (called a 'trill'). *Brrrr-rllppp, brrrrllppp, brrrrup, brrrup!* On and on they honked those sounds in repeat. She knew her brent goose dreams were significant as, in Celtic Christianity, the wild goose is a symbol of the Holy Spirit. This came from days when the Greylag Goose ('Gé ghlas' in Irish) represented the Holy Spirit. The Greylag goose lived at Brónach's home, as well as the rest of Britain. Over time, any wild goose species represented the Holy Spirit. Now, Brónach knew the brent geese overwintered in the loughs of Co. Down (both Strangford Lough and Carlingford Lough), so which lough should she go to?

Then she had another dream, of walking past the huge Cloughmore Stone near Rostrevor, Co. Down, to the south of the Mourne Mountains. Everyone in Ulster at that time knew the story of how it got there. It was a huge granite bolder, sitting on the slopes of Slieve Martin Mountain that overlooked the forests of Rostrevor and Carlingford Lough. The giant, Fionn mac Cumhaill (Finn McCool), had been having a battle one day with another giant, and thrown it at him from the Cooley Mountains in Co. Louth, all the way northwards across Carlingford Lough! Some say that the other giant was the Scottish giant, Benandonner; others say it was a local frost-giant named Ruiscairre. The locals rightly called the Cloughmore Stone 'the big stone'.

Well, that settled it. God's plan for her was to set up a church near Carlingford Lough. Through her dreams and visions, and even little 'pictures' in her head, God had left a trail of pebbles for Brónach, like in the *Hansel and Gretel* story, to find the way to her new home. One of these pebbles was even a huge, 50-tonne bolder!

So Brónach lived beside the stormy waters of Carlingford Lough, on its north side in what is now Co. Down. She started a church for the local people and chose a beautiful site right under Slieve Martin Mountain and the Cloughmore Stone of her dream. It overlooked a lovely river and glen. Its old name was Glen Sechis ('the Glen of Seclusion'), so it was a perfect place to meditate on God. In the future, it would be named after her – Cell Brónche ('church of Brónach'), now Kilbroney. Today, the modern village of Rostrevor is beside it.

Brónach frequently meditated and prayed, 'Dear God, how can I get the people to stop believing in the druids' teaching about Manannán mac Lir? I want them to know that you will take care of them when they are at sea. And how can I make sure that my life is not "sorrowful"? I want to help people, God!'

Carlingford Lough's waters were very dangerous at times. An earlier name for that lough was Snám Aignech ('swift sea-channel, ford'). Swift, meaning fast. You see, because the sea entered through a narrow inlet, currents could be fast and strong during storms. Brónach decided to warn the fishermen and sailors about any approaching storms.

Brónach also commissioned St Patrick's bell maker to make her a bell also. Her little bell ('cloc' in Old Irish, or 'clog' in modern Irish) was made by St Mac Céacht. Brónach used the bell to summon her nuns to the convent. Also, she looked at the sky every day. She often went down to the lough to watch the brent geese, to see if the birds' behaviour might indicate a storm was on the way. If it looked like bad weather was coming, she would walk up the headland further up Slieve Martin and look out over Carlingford Lough. *Ding, ding...ding, ding!* Long, clear and hard she rung her bell, its clapper striking loudly. She used her bell often, and soon she had a church full of grateful sailors and their families!

These people had believed that Manannán mac Lir would take them to the Otherworld by drowning them at sea. But Brónach spoke truths from the Bible that she had memorised by heart. God from the Bible would keep His people safe, not drown them. God also certainly did not need to be feared or appeased with offerings, like the druids taught about the sea god.

As well as her church, it is said Brónach built a refuge for the sailors who were shipwrecked in the lough. There, she taught them about the forgiveness of God in a way that everyone could understand, but also in a way that the fishermen could specifically understand. She used Bible verses such as this one:

> *You will again have compassion on us; you will tread our sins underfoot and*
> *hurl all our iniquities into the depths of the sea.*
> – Micah 7:19, NIV

It is said that Brónach went on to have children. She must have been a great mother, as we know all of these children became church leaders. However, some of them were born and died so much later than Brónach that it's impossible she was the mum of all of them. Nevertheless, here are their six names:

- ❋ **St Mo Chaoi/Caolán of Nendrum** (d. 497). He founded a monastery further north of Kilbroney and Rostrevor, on Mahee Island in Strangford Lough. This is also in Co. Down.

- ❋ **St Fursa/Fursey** (d. 650). He spread Christianity through East Anglia in England and then France.

- ❋ **St Colmán Comraire of Uisneach**, Co. Westmeath.

- ❋ **St Colmán Muilinn**. He founded the Church of Derrykeighan in Co. Antrim.

- ❋ **St Mac Erca**, a bishop. He might have founded the Church of Donaghmore, Co. Down.

- ❋ **St Damhnad**. She was the female founder of the Church of Tech Damnatan/Tydavent, Sliab Betha, Co. Monaghan. Her staff ('bachall' in Irish) was said to have been used as a lie detector! It is now in the National Museum of Ireland. She is not to be confused with St Dymphna of Geel, Belgium. The feast day for St Damhnad is the 13th June.

When Brónach was older, it is said that Vikings invaded Kilbroney! She was brave right up to the end and stood up to the Viking chief, but he attacked her. He hit her head very hard, and she was sadly killed. But then, the story goes to say that where her blood fell, a holy well of pure spring water sprang up. This well is still present today in the Kilbroney churchyard. Many people still go there and pray that God would use the water as a cure for throat and eyesight problems.

Brónach's life turned out to be anything but sorrowful. She was one of the few female saints to have a crosier (bishop's staff), as her brother Gall died before her and she was made its custodian. When she died, a cross was placed over her grave at Kilbroney. Today there is a cross there made of granite from the nearby Mourne Mountains. It shows the importance of her and her church.

But what became of her famous bell? There is a story that for hundreds of years after the church, a bell could be heard ringing on stormy nights. Locals remembered that it must still be a warning to seafarers on Carlingford Lough. It was also thought that the sound came from the old graveyard – though some said it was just banshees or fairies. Some might have thought it was a screech from a Graveyard Screamer or Screecher (known in English as a barn owl, or in Irish as a Scréachóg Reilige'). But no, it was clearly the sound of a bell. In 1839, over 184 years ago, a storm brought down a large old oak tree in the graveyard. In its branches, there was a tenth-century bell (perhaps dating to 900 AD)! The bell is now in the nearby Star of the Sea Church, Rostrevor. If you visit the church, a striker rings the bell for you so that you can hear it! It sounds a perfect pitch 'D'. Was it placed in the tree to save it during Viking raids? We will never know!

57

St Bronagh's Shrine

Rose Brennan © 2015

She came onto our shores and she settled on our land,
With a calling she would follow God`s command,
She heard him whisper on the wind that blew the breeze,
At her shrine we pray on bended knee.

She set her church upon Kilbroney's rolling fields,
She spread the Christian word in gospel and in deed,
She tended castaways washed up on the bay,
And the people came to worship and to pray.

Chorus
The sick and the poor, the lame and the blind,
All gathered in prayer at St Bronagh`s dear shrine,
With cares in our heart and prayers on our mind,
As we kneel before St Bronagh`s shrine.

She walked the village and she prayed among the hills,
She went into their homes and she nursed the people's ills,
She blessed the children and she tended to the poor,
And her story would be told for evermore.

We celebrate her feast as the daffodils push through,
In the springtime we will sing St Bronagh`s tune,
Her shrine adorned with flowers, holy water in her well,
Blessed lady, ring out loud St Bronagh`s bell.

Chorus
The sick and the poor, the lame and the blind,
All gathered in prayer at St Bronagh`s dear shrine,
With cares in our heart and prayers on our mind,
As we kneel before St Bronagh`s shrine.

For Celtic Christians, the Holy Spirit was described as a wild goose. If you had to compare God to any animal (including birds), which animal would it be? For example, a lion (king)! See how many you can list or draw, with a reason why for each.

DID YOU KNOW?

❋ **Feast Day:** 2nd April.

❋ **Other names:** Bronagh.

❋ According to Reserve Manager, Maurice Turley, of WWW Castle Espie, at present there are about 700 overwintering, light-bellied brent geese on Carlingford Lough.

❋ Stained glass windows of Brónach often show her with her bell and crosier. E.g., Ballyholme Church of Ireland and Rostrevor Chapel. She is also shown in All Saints Roman Catholic Church, Ballymena, just with her crosier.

❋ The first new Benedictine Abbey of monks for 800 years (in Northern Ireland) was built in the valley of St Bronagh's Church in Rostrevor.

❋ The Kilbroney Centre is a Christian Residential and Conference Centre in Rostrevor, Co. Down. It holds super children's summer camps!

❋ There is St Bronagh's Primary School and St Bronagh's GAA, both in Rostrevor.

❋ The Broighter Hoard of gold objects (including a boat) can be seen in the National Museum of Ireland, Dublin. They date to the first century BC and were discovered near Limavady, Co. Derry, in 1896. It has been suggested that they were offerings to the sea god, Manannán mac Lir.

❋ Kilbroney Park was visited by the writer Charles Dickens. It was also visited by the writer C. S. Lewis and may have helped provide inspiration for the land of Narnia!

Beautiful Buriana

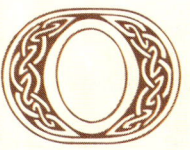nce upon a time, long ago, a decree was issued in a palace in the south of Ireland. The announcement was made by the father of a beautiful princess. It went: 'Buriana, my daughter, your beauty is unmatched throughout Munster. You are of age to marry now, so I have decided that I will organise for you to wed the most brave and handsome prince out of all the best royalty that we can find!' Buriana sighed: 'Oh dear, I don't want to be a part of yet another princess story where the bride has to find true love from a prince, or anything even close to that!' Buriana had done lots of reading, you see. She was not only lovely to look at but highly intelligent.

Buriana was indeed a stunning princess. Her father was a king in Munster, the province in the south of Ireland. But, like so many Irish Christians, she longed to help spread her faith. One night, she ran in secret from the palace to the coast! From there, she sailed across the rough Irish and Celtic Seas in a currach. We don't know for sure if she took others with her but, being a rich princess (and quite sensible), she probably did. (Perhaps just a select few who wouldn't announce it to her father). Buriana prayed that the winds and currents would be directed by God, until finally they had safely landed at a little port called Penzance in Cornwall. If you've heard of Land's End, well it was only a short distance from there too. It was on the southwest tip of what is now southwest England.

As soon as the locals saw her arrive, they asked Buriana where she had come from. She told them all about herself and the people said, 'We'll call you Berriona.' You see, the old Latin name for Ireland in the fifth-sixth century was Hiberione, which gives us Hi beriona, which literally means 'the Irish lady'. In Cornish, which is the language spoken in Cornwall, the name then became Beryona or Beryon.

Buriana travelled 5 miles (8.0 km) west, then set up her base. She taught the people about Christ, looked after the poor, and prayed to help heal the sick. It wasn't long before word got around the whole kingdom about this... That kingdom was called Dumnonia and it covered Cornwall, Devon and some parts of Somerset. Even the king of Dumnonia, King Gerailt, had his son brought to her. His son couldn't walk, but after Buriana prayed for him, he was cured of his paralysis!

You would think the king would be grateful, but gratitude turned to greed and he decided that he would make her his prize. Now, you see, King Gerailt was known as a valiant warrior. We have records of his battle wins. Poetry was even written about him. He was a man used to getting what he wanted; he took things by the power of his sword. So, before Buriana knew it, she was kidnapped. Now she was locked up at the King's stronghold at Trevorgans.

All Buriana's friends, including St Piran, an Irish monk who had also travelled over to Cornwall, hurried as fast as they could to the castle to beg for her release. King Gerailt just laughed and thought to himself, 'what challenge will I set these Irish Christians?' You see, even though his son had been miraculously healed, he still didn't believe in their faith himself. He thought long and hard for something difficult, yes, impossible even. 'I will release Buriana to you if in the morning I am woken by the sound of a cuckoo calling in the snow.' It was ludicrous!

You see, the common cuckoo ('Cuach' in Irish) spends the winter in Africa and only in the summer does it migrate to Europe. Of course, you know that it only snows in winter (with the exception of late autumn and early spring). It was impossible to hear a cuckoo when it was snowing! It was late October in Cornwall in our story, and there was neither snow nor a cuckoo about.

As this verse from a poem shows, which is supposed to have been written by the hero Fionn mac Cumhaill (Finn McCool), the cuckoo only comes in summer!

> Now comes the bird of dusty hue,
>> The loud cuckoo, the summer-lover;
> Branching trees are thick with leaves;
>> The bitter, evil time is over.*

* Taken from The High Deeds of Finn and other Bardic Romances of Ancient Ireland, by Irish writer T. W. Rolleston (d. 1920).

So, what happened next in the story? Well, St Piran and their companions stood all night praying outside the walls of the castle. And slowly but surely, it started to snow. And to make things even more special, it snowed everywhere except where the group of Buriana's friends stood! Then, as the sun started to come up, King Gerailt distinctly heard a *cuckcoo*, *cuckoo* from inside his castle.

Gerailt was struck by fear and quickly summoned the group outside to come get Buriana. He asked for their forgiveness and handed Buriana over to them. In Ireland, at least, it was believed that if you heard a cuckoo from indoors, say through an open window or door, it meant very bad luck was coming your way. We don't know what beliefs about the cuckoo existed in Cornwall in the fifth-sixth century, but Gerailt was still petrified as, given the task he had set, it seemed impossible.

So, happily, Buriana and her friends set off home; only, when they had almost arrived, it turned out that Gerailt had changed his mind. He thought to himself, 'Maybe this is just some sort of wizardry...' With that thought, he and some of his soldiers went after Buriana. It was something similar to the story in the Old Testament part of the Bible, about Moses and the Israelites. The Israelites had been kept as slaves for many years but the Egyptian king, the Pharoah, allowed them to leave after God sent the ten plagues against the Egyptians. After, however, the Pharoah changed his mind and raced after them to the Red Sea.

Now, as Gerailt himself reached out to make Buriana his prisoner again, she DIED! Now, that might seem like a strange ending, but it is not the final ending of Buriana's story. For Piran and the band of Christian friends all prayed – and Buriana's life was miraculously restored. That was the final miracle that was needed to make Gerailt and his whole family become Christian believers. And with the King a believer, Buriana had his patronage and support to tell even more people about Christ.

When Buriana did finally die, she was buried at her church. A village grew up around it and is now called St Buryan, after the name that she was given when she arrived in Cornwall. Many miracles occurred at her grave. One day, an even more famous king, King Æthelstan (d. 939 AD), stopped at St Buriana's Chapel while on his way to battle against the Scilly Isles (off the southwest coast of Cornwall). He took communion, said a prayer to St Buriana, and promised that if he were victorious he would build a splendid church on that site. Indeed, his campaign proved successful and, on his return, he kept his promise. He issued a royal charter and built a magnificent church at St Buryan, which had special status directly under his jurisdiction for many centuries. Even this king, the first king of the whole of England, asked Buriana for help. And so, the town was blessed through her even until today, as people from all over the world travel to see where she lived and helped people.

More than a beautiful face...

TASK

There are a lot of beautiful princesses in this book. But can you give some practical examples of what is more important to God than a beautiful face?

O worship the LORD in the beauty of holiness.
Psalm 96:9a, KJV

DID YOU KNOW?

❊ **Feast days:** Sunday closest to 13th May (old May Day in the Julian calendar), 1st May, 29th May, and 4th & 19th June (not celebrated anymore).

❊ **Other names:** Berriona, Beriana, Beryan and Buryan.

❊ Some people think Buriana is the same saint as St Bruinsech of Mag Trea/ Clonguish, Co. Longford, whose Feast Day is 29th May, but this is uncertain. There is almost the same story about St Bruinsech, but the cuckoo is replaced by a heron. Also, in that version the King's castle is burnt down as a punishment (though his son is safe).

❊ In some versions, Buriana stays dead for her own protection against the King.

❊ The cuckoo is famous for laying eggs in the nests of other smaller birds, especially dunnocks, meadow pipits and reed warblers. Indeed, this is so common with the Meadow Pipit that some of its Irish names reflect this. 'Banaltra na Cuaiche' means 'Nurse of the Cuckoo', and 'Giolla na Cuaiche' means 'Servant of the Cuckoo'. The cuckoo also sometimes lays its eggs in the nests of pied wagtails, robins and sedge warblers. The cuckoo chick is then raised by its new 'parents' but is *much* larger than them and the parent birds don't realise they have been misled!

❊ Arthur Langdon, in 1896 AD, recorded twelve lovely old crosses in St Buryan parish, one of which is in the churchyard.

Constant Cainer

All her life, Cainer never gave up when she set her mind on something. Her father, Cruithnechán of Cell Cuilinn in Carbery (Cairbre), Co. Cork, was always praising her for that quality. When she decided to become a nun and founded her convent at Bantry (Benntraige), also in Co. Cork, she was determined to be the best nun she could be. Co. Cork is in the province of Munster, in the south of Ireland. Cainer did all the things nuns do; she persistently prayed, looked after the destitute and sick every day, always showed abstinence in tasty treats, and often fervently fasted (even going with nothing to eat at all sometimes)! Cainer set an excellent example to others of being consistently constant in the faith. And so it went her whole life. So holy was she that her nickname of sorts was Cainer Cráibdech, meaning 'holy' or 'pious' (in Old Irish). Imagine having 'holy' or 'pious' as the second part of your doubled-barrelled name. However, our story about Cainer is really about one particular story when she was an elderly lady.

One night, Cainer was praying after nocturns (the prayer service at night), when she had an amazing vision. There before her, as clear as day, she saw the whole of Ireland covered with its churches. A tower of fire rose up from each of them. She could see her own church down in the very south of Ireland. However, her eye was drawn north, about a quarter of the way up the island of Ireland. She looked up to where the tallest flame of them all rose up. The flame looked as if it was going straight up to the stars and heaven! Cainer realised that she was looking at Scattery Island (Inis Cathaigh), Co. Clare. That great famous monastery was on an island in the mouth of the mighty River Shannon's estuary. The River Shannon is the longest river in Ireland, so she could trace its journey in her mind's eye right to its mouth where it met the sea. And there Scattery Island was at its mouth, where it entered the Atlantic Ocean. In her vision, Scattery Island's round tower looked

65

taller than the others. In reality, Cainer knew it was one of the tallest in Ireland, but she also knew it wasn't *the* tallest.

Immediately Cainer knew what her vision meant. What she actually said in antiquated English was, 'Fair is yon cell... Thither will I go, that my resurrection may be near it.' (A 'cell' was a church, monastery, convent etc.). By this, what she meant was: 'That is an amazing church...That's where I want to go to die and depart to heaven from.' Straightaway, Cainer set off on her journey. She didn't have a map or compass (never mind the Internet on a modern mobile phone); the only guidance she had was her vision. The tower of fire at Scattery Island kept blazing tall and straight up to the stars and heaven as it had done. It never went out; it blazed night and day. It was an extremely long journey for an old lady, but eventually Cainer arrived in Limerick (Luimnech).

There was a bustling little port there at the mouth of the mighty River Shannon. Large boats and small currachs were tied up, coming in and out. Cainer crossed over to the island in the centre of the river (what Ptolemy labelled as 'Regia' on his 150 AD map of Ireland). I like to think that Cainer had some food and something to drink after her long journey. I think the many people of Limerick would have enquired about where she had come from. Maybe she used the opportunity to tell them about her purpose in coming there, and perhaps she even prophesied about a certain young monk called Munchin (Mainchín), who would start a monastery in Limerick. Or our other 'amazing Irish woman', St Íte of Killeedy in Co. Limerick, who would come along.

However, knowing that her vision of the round tower on Scattery Island never stopped, it wouldn't surprise me if she didn't take a break at Limerick after all. Elderly Cainer stepped out onto the river. Yes, *onto* the river! What that first step was like, I can only guess. Sometimes, there is a tidal bore on the Shannon, which is where a large wave sweeps up the river estuary from the Atlantic Ocean and up past Limerick. But not that day. Cainer was unwavering and the waves were calm that day. And she walked on water, just like Jesus did on Lake Galilee.

It was a marathon of a walk out from Limerick to Scattery Island. The Shannon estuary is 60 miles (97 km) long from Limerick to the Atlantic Ocean. Scattery Island is about 50 miles (80.47 km) from Limerick. There are organised walks nowadays that distance and people do well if they can complete them within twenty hours – that is about a day and night! So Cainer walked by day and Cainer walked by night, and she walked a second day (as she was very old). But, supernaturally empowered, she walked on and on. It was as if invisible angels were helping her too.

She went past lots of little islands near Limerick as she paced on to the southwest. On the second day, she was very close. The estuary turned west.

The tower of fire before her that she knew was Scattery Island was right in front of her. People from Kilrush on the northern shore of the mainland could see her (and Kilrush was only 1.86 miles (3 km) from Scattery Island, so they could see everything). Some fishermen who were out in their currachs catching the herrings and throwing out their nets for the salmon had an even better view of events. What an amazing sight it was. Cainer had 'crossed the sea with dry feet as if she were on smooth land', as it was written in the *Book of Lismore*. For, God is 'able to do immeasurably more than all we ask or imagine, according to his power that is at work within us' (Ephesians 3:20, NIV).

St Senán, who was head of the monastery of Scattery Island, was a deeply prophetic, miracle-working monk. He didn't need to look out any of the nine windows in Scattery Island's tower; he had heard from God all about Cainer's journey and was expecting her! St Senán walked along down to the harbour and greeted the wonder-working woman. 'Yes, I've come,' said Cainer, as if they knew each other well as old friends and were used to starting their conversations in the middle. But St Senán said, 'Go to your sister who lives in that island to the east, that you might be a guest there.'

Now, it's not entirely understood what St Senán meant, but some people think he might have been Cainer's nephew, and it was his mother who was Cuman, Cainer's sister, who was nearby. However, that interpretation is not 'clear cut', as they say. Other people think that Senán and Cainer were brother and sister, and that Cuman was mother of them both.

But back to our story, Cainer then said to Senán. 'Not for that have we come, but that I might stay with you on this island.' I like the way she said, 'we', as if referring to God being with her. Senán said, 'Women don't enter this island.' You see, Senán was leader of a community of male monks; no women were allowed on Scattery Island. Cainer replied, 'How can you say that? Christ is no worse than you. Christ came to redeem women, no less than to redeem men. He did not suffer less for the sake of women than for the sake of men. Women have given humble service and ministered to Christ and to his Apostles. Women then, no less than men, enter into the Kingdom of Heaven. Why, then, would you not take women to you onto your island?'

Senán replied back to her with a brief, 'You are stubborn!' Taking that as a 'yes', Cainer said: 'What then, shall I get what I asked for, a place for my side on this island and the sacrament from you to me?' By the 'sacrament', she meant Holy

Communion (or Mass). Senán understood what Cainer meant by 'a place for my side'; she was asking for a burial plot for herself. Senán knew she was elderly and it was her time to die. So Senán said, 'A place of resurrection will be given you here on the brink of the wave, but I fear that the sea will carry off your remains.' By this, he meant he would only allow her to be buried in the intertidal zone (the area between high and low tides, which would sometimes be covered by water).

Cainer said, 'God will grant me that the spot where I will lie will not be the first that the sea will bear away.' Therefore, Senán gave her permission to step on to the shore of the island. The whole time they had been talking Cainer had been standing on a wave, with her staff under one arm as if she was on land. When she came ashore, Senán gave her Holy Communion (or Mass), and straightaway Cainer went to heaven. According to what was agreed, Senán and his monks took care of Cainer's body and saw that she was buried. To stay true to his own church laws, it is said that Senán waited until low tide to bury her in the inter-tidal zone, which was not officially the 'island', so he could fulfil Cainer's wish without breaking his own rules.

There is a local story that a flagstone, called locally 'Leac na ban beannuighe' ('the stone of the holy woman' or 'the saintly woman's stone') was put over Cainer's grave. It is said locally that it is only seen at low tide every seven years. The legend is that whoever sees the flagstone will get whatever request he or she desires.

Having said that, Cainer's grave is called 'Lady's grave', and is the fourth prayer station of the eleven stations around Scattery Island. These rounds of stations are performed on Easter Monday or St Senán's Day (8th March).

It is also written that God granted to Cainer that anyone who visited her church before going to sea would never drown before going and returning. So, St Cainer is the patron saint of fishermen and seafarers.

So, should women and girls visit Scattery Island today? Absolutely! But if you visit the reputed burial site of St Senán on Scattery Island (a small oratory called St Senan's Bed), across the top of the entrance there is a metal bar. Some believe this was put there to remind those who are female not to enter. As according to folklore, girls or women who go inside will become barren (they won't be able to have children)!

But we must not think that St Senán was against women. He founded two convents for nuns and was visiting one of them when he died.

Nowadays, there are no monks (or anyone) living on Scattery Island. The last residents left it in the year 1969. If you would live to visit it, you can sail there by boat in the summer months, as there are trips leaving from Kilrush marina.

Don't let gender get in the way!

TASK

Cainer was always constant and never gave up, even when women weren't 'allowed' to do something. Make a list of things that you would like to do when you are older. Perhaps you would like to be a builder, car mechanic, plumber, doctor, physicist, chemist, astronaut, electrician, farmer, vet or mathematician! These are jobs that were mainly done by men in the past. Don't let gender get in the way! Make your list of what you might like to do.

DID YOU KNOW?

❋ Feast day: 28th January.

❋ Other names: Canir, Cainnear, Cannera, Canair, Conainne, Canaire, Connera, Kinnera and Cainder.

❋ Thomas Moore (1779-1852) was a famous Irish poet. He also wrote lyrics to songs. One of those is called 'St Senanus and the Lady', which is about St Cainer.

❋ The highest round tower in Ireland is at Kilmacduagh, Co. Galway. It is 34.5 m (113 ft) tall! The round tower on Scattery Island, Co. Clare, is 26 metres (85 ft) tall now – the round tower in Cainer's vision appeared taller to symbolise the power of God there. A little part of its cap at the top is missing (maybe struck by lightning).

❋ The round tower at Scattery Island is unusual in that its door is at ground level. It is the only one like that besides the one at Castledermot in Co. Kildare.

❋ My story is based on the round tower that is still present on Scattery Island. However, it is dated to have been built during the tenth-eleventh centuries, after Cainer's story.

Crazy Cranat

'reat Balor of the Evil Eye, Cranat! What have you done, sister?' This was said while onlookers nearly passed out with shock and Cranat's nuns scurried about in the trees. Cranat's brother continued, 'What have you done to your beautiful face, Cranat? Do you want to be a one-eyed monster?' So, who was Balor of the Evil Eye, who was Cranat, and why did she cause such consternation to her brother?

Long, long ago in the myths of old Ireland, long before there were any saints, there were stories of the gods and goddesses, and Formorians. The Fomorians were a supernatural race; hostile, monstrous beings who came from under the sea, or the earth. Sometimes, they were seen as giants and sea raiders. Whatever way they were portrayed, they were the enemies of Ireland's gods and goddesses (the Tuatha Dé Danann). One particularly nasty Fomorian was called Balor of the Evil Eye; he was their leader for a time. He was a giant, with a huge, single eye in his head, which wreaked death and destruction whenever opened. Yes, his eye had the supernatural power to kill! Now, that is not unnecessary information for our story, for it paints a picture of how having only one eye would have been viewed in old Ireland. One eye wasn't pretty. It wasn't a quality to be desired. Indeed, even today, the story that follows is downright crazy and utterly strange! For one particular girl though, called Cranat, it seemed to make no difference that the most famous grotesque Irish monster had just one eye.

Let me tell you about Cranat. Cranat was a gutsy girl who grew up in Co. Cork, in the kingdom of Fermoy. Co. Cork is in the province of Munster, in the south of Ireland. Right from when she was young, Cranat showed grit; if she set her mind to something, she did it! It is said that she had two full brothers, Breanat (or Beircheart) and Nicholas. Their father was called Buicín, so Cranat's full name was

Cranat ingen Buicín. Her half-brother (through her mother) was called Fínán, and he was King of Fir Maige Féne (later known as Fermoy) in Co. Cork.

When it came time for Cranat to marry, her half-brother, King Fínán, thought that Cranat would be pleased with the many suitors he had lined up to see her. Cranat was very beautiful, so there were lots of suitors. A prince of Munster was extremely interested in marrying Cranat, however the only thing that Cranat wanted to do was lead a holy life and be a nun. Indeed, it would seem from details mentioned in our story that Cranat already led a community of nuns. Now, as I've said, Cranat was known for her spirited personality and tenacity. She never gave up!

The Munster suitor was called Cairbre Crom (d. 578/580), the son of Criomhthann. The story is told that when this prince heard that the beautiful Cranat wouldn't marry him, his family decided to take Cranat by force! Their kingdom neighboured her half-brother's and they were a dangerous rival. So it was a tricky situation diplomatically. Never did Cranat and her family guess what was going to happen though. Cairbre Crom's family sent a band of kidnappers to Cranat's home. Cranat despaired at what to do. There was no way she was going to be forced into an unwanted marriage, especially through kidnap. 'Categorically, completely, *no*... I will *never* marry him!' Cranat exploded. In desperation, Cranat decided to get rid of her beautiful looks and as fast as she could, and with a lot of effort, she plucked out *both* her eyes from their sockets! Now, it would seem she didn't just look like Balor the leader of the Fomorians, she had *no eyes*!

After pulling out her eyes, Cranat thoroughly cursed her colluding brother, Fínán, though she didn't curse the kingship away from him. Cranat also made sure that he paid her money towards the churches in Fermoy.

So, what became of Cranat's eyes? In one version of the story, it is said that she placed her eyes into the hands of two of her nuns, Máel Bracha and Laithche. Can you just imagine their shock?

In a different version of the story, instead of handing them to her two nuns, it is said that where one of Cranat's eyes landed (at Annakisha North in Clenor parish), an ash tree grew. It became known as Crannahulla (or Crann a'Shúile, Tree of the Eye). It is also told that a twig from this tree was reputed to be a charm against shipwreck and drowning. Because of this, the bark of it was stripped by the huge numbers of emigrants leaving Ireland in the nineteenth century. By the 1860s, there was hardly any of the tree left. The tree was also considered to be incombustible, as wood from it would not burn. As a result, the ash tree is now gone, with no trace of it left. There was also said to have been a second tree venerated, but nothing more is known about it. Perhaps it grew where the second eye landed?

And did Cranat go the rest of her life without her eyes? Well, no. There is a story that her nun, Laithche, scrambled around in a tree to find one of her eyes. She found it, but there were bits of barks stuck to the socket! Cranat popped it back into her eye socket and miraculously she could see again, but it is said that she had a rather fierce look after that. As for the other eye, we are given no details in the story, but I presume they found it too.

It says in the Bible:

> For the eyes of the Lord range throughout the earth to strengthen those whose hearts are fully committed to him.
> – 2 Chronicles 16:9a, NIV

Can you imagine God's eyes roaming the whole world looking for people to help? In King James' version of the Bible, it says God's eyes 'run to and fro throughout the whole earth'! Well, with all her complete craziness, Cranat was seen by God and strengthened by Him. She then went on to found a church in Co. Cork. Maybe it was crazy and a bit unconventional too. And she is especially remembered in lots of other locations in the south of Ireland.

Cranat's craziness

In what specific ways could you put into practice some of Cranat's craziness, in a good way? Have perseverance, drive and guts? Be dedicated, assertive and firm? Be specific!

DID YOU KNOW?

* Feast day: 9th March.

* Other names: Cránaid, Crannat, Cranit, Craebhnat, Craobhnad and Crawnat.

* Holy Wells: Garranachole townland (used occasionally) and Kilcranathan (abandoned).

* If you have read the other stories in this book, can you remember who else pulled out their eye or eyes?

* According to @eDIL_Dictionary in the Dinneen's dictionary, the moon was once known in Irish as 'súil Bhalair' ('Balor's eye').

* Some people disagree with Balor having just one deadly eye. They think that he might have had one or even two other normal ones (as well as the dangerous eye)!

Dazzling Dahalin

Before sunrise, in old Ireland, it was common for raiders (or pirates as they are more often called) to swoop on unsuspecting villages! With cutlasses drawn, those raiders were terrifying. They would often take people captive and sell them to others. It wasn't unusual to be taken far from your home and never see your family again. Proper pirates were not on interesting adventures with a treasure map, carrying their talking Polly parrot, saying, 'Ahoy matey!'

One such encounter with real pirates was with a girl called Dahalin. Dahalin lived in the fifth and sixth century, Co. Kerry, in the southwest of Ireland. In the time Dahalin lived, pirates were common. Dahalin was a nun, and her church was off the coast road on the north side of Kerry Head. It was about 3 miles (4.8 km) north of Ballyheigue village on a hillside. She and her other nuns had a lovely view of the Atlantic Ocean from their little wooden church. But Dahalin had the gift of prophecy, and one night the view was not so lovely. In her mind's eye, she saw a dangerous band of raiders approaching her church. Perhaps they had seen a light in the church from their ship below. Not afraid of their weapons or of being kidnapped, she went out to meet them head on! No one was going to make a slave out of her and her nuns.

Some records of the story say they were rough wayward boys. And there are other later versions that include feared Vikings, Normans and Cromwellians. There are even specifically stories of Mountjoy's men, the hated Lord Deputy of Ireland in Queen Elizabeth I's time (and later Lord Lieutenant of Ireland under King James VI and I). However, it is unlikely that they were just boys and all of the other suggestions are too late for Dahalin's time. The most reliable story is that they were pirates or raiders. Regardless of what they were, they were dangerous. However,

75

Dahalin knew immediately what to do. As light dazzled in her own eyes, she prayed, and they were struck blind with the power of God shining out from her.

Not only were the raiders struck blind, they were also struck with fear! Like scared boys they scrambled along the hillside, groping their way on the grass. But Dahalin, confident that God would protect her, felt sorry them. She said that if they repented and promised to change their ways she would undo their blindness. She must have known the true state of their hearts. Though there is a version of the story where there were three of them, and that they were soldiers instead of raiders. Two of them kept their promise, but one backtracked and tried to grab Dahalin! That one, Dahalin blinded for a second time. In most versions of the story though, they all promised and kept to it.

There are three versions of how the pirates got their sight back. In one, Dahalin went over to a rock and tipped it, and water came out. In another version, she scooped up some earth and water came out. In a third tale, there was a well of water already in existence and Dahalin told them to make their way over to it and bathe their eyes in it. In each story, they were healed when their eyes touched the water!

St Dahalin's well still exists, about 400 metres (0.25 miles) from St Dahlin's church (Teampall Daithleann). The well is fittingly called Tobar na Súl ('Well of the Eyes'). It became famous for healing eye problems and is still an extremely popular holy well to visit. The story of the raiders and how Dahalin blinded them and then healed them is told on a plaque beside the well. The exact words on the plaque are:

> *This well is named after St Dahillan, who is reputed to have stricken blind would-be despoilers of her convent. On undertaking to decease their molestations, she told them that to regain their eyesight they were to bathe their eyes in the well. They did so and their sight was restored. According to tradition the well still retains this miraculous quality.*

Another remarkable thing about St Dahalin's holy well is that it is said a trout lives in it. The legend about this says that if anyone see this trout and makes a wish, it is always granted! However, very few get the privilege of seeing the trout.

There is also the story of mad Crosbie, and as quite often happens in stories, there is more than one version. Long ago in the seventeenth century, after St Dahalin, there lived a well-known man called Crosbie in the nearby village of Ballyheigue. He was one of the Cromwellian soldiers who helped conquer

Ireland and, for that reason, he got the largest tract of land in Ballyheigue and became landlord of the whole parish. He hated the poor of the area and how they relied on holy wells instead of paying for a doctor. Well, one day he heard of Tobar na Súl, Well of the Eyes, but he didn't believe that there was any cure in its waters. So, to make fun of the well, he took out his three dogs and set off for the well. When he reached it, with contempt, he threw one of his dogs into it! No sooner did he do so, it began to howl so loud that he had to pull it out again. When he did so, it swelled up and died almost immediately. The silly man then threw in his second dog and the same thing happened! Same with his third! Three dead dogs lay at his feet now. It was as if a curse had fallen upon him, for he started to bark, he started to howl, and until the day of his death he wandered Ireland like that! Insane. It is said that from that day to today in Co. Kerry, people would never interfere with a holy well ever again, nor refuse a priest a request (Adapted from 'Holy Wells Cork and Kerry' blog).

In another version of that story, told by the writer Clodagh Finn, Crosbie, known as 'Láimhín' Crosbie, allowed his Kerry Blue terrier to splash around in the water (just one dog, not three). Touching the holy water, his dog became rabid with the disease called rabies and bit Crosbie. Crosbie in this version of the story was up on a wall barking like a dog! The 'curse' followed him to the afterlife, as people saw his ghost wandering the countryside, barking as he went. His nickname Láimhín means 'little hand', as even though it was hundreds of years after her death, St Dahalin, or God, withered his hand for his blasphemous actions. Rabies is a terrible disease and one quite ironic symptom of the illness is fear of water. Crosbie certainly wouldn't be going near any holy wells once he had been bitten!

On the other hand, there is the story of a woman who went to the well to fill a pot for cooking. When she realised the water wouldn't boil, she returned it to the well. However, she wasn't punished. The message is that God knows the heart and one's motives.

Traditionally, the well is visited on a Friday or Saturday. Other popular times for visiting include May Day, midsummer in June, and Michaelmas (29th September). Three rounds of the well are made while saying the rosary. People often drink the water from the well and sometimes they rub it on a part of their body that needs healing. Often something is left at the well, e.g. money or holy pictures.

Dahalin was said to be the sister of the monk, St Erc mac Dega of Slane. Indeed, St Erc has a holy well not far from St Dahalin's Well of the Eyes. And if she was St Erc's sister, then she was also a sister of St Ia ('Intrepid Ia').

The area around St Dahalin's church and well is known as Glendahalin, Dahalin's Glen. The present ruins of Dahalin's tiny church building are from the eighth century. The ruins are not the actual building that Dahalin would have spent her time in (she and her nuns would have had a wooden church), but it is lovely to see the eighth-century building that is on the same site as Dahalin's original church.

So you might ask, what happened next to those pirates? Well, I like to think that they became really friendly 'saintly' seafarers after that! Dahalin no doubt taught them at least some Bible verses. Pirates love treasure, so here is a Bible verse that pirates would understand:

> *Of all the people on earth, the Lord your God has chosen you to be his own special treasure.*
> – Deuteronomy 7:6b, NLT

Then, instead of pillaging people, the pirates took to the high oceans, had fun looking for mermaids, and never ever made anyone walk the plank again!

Yo Ho, Yo Ho! A pirate's life for me!

TASK

Oh-or, oh-or! Write a pirate story! Pillage as many pirate phrases as you can (parrot, eye-patch, peg-leg, deserted island, walking the plank, pirate language, gold, ship's captain, cabin boy). Is your story going to have a moral to it? Be sure to illustrate it with your own labelled treasure map!

DID YOU KNOW?

- ❉ **Feast day:** 4th June.
- ❉ **Other names:** St Daithlionn, Daithleann, Dathalan, Dahillan and Daithle.
- ❉ Facts from Clodagh Finn:
    - One year, a choir from Switzerland with Alpine horns sung at Dahalin's church!
    - The Wild Atlantic Way and North Kerry Way walking trail now pass Dahalin's church and the Well of the Eyes. It will become an even more popular place of pilgrimage.

Determined Darbiled

It was extremely early one June morning on a Friday in Kells, Co. Meath. Two teachers, Mrs. Wilson and Mrs. Neeson, stood at the front of the class with an assortment of willing parents. Today was no ordinary day. Today was a school trip to Co. Mayo! They were going to visit St Darbiled's church ruins and hear her story. It would be a long journey, from the far east to the far west of Ireland, so their departure time was hours before school would normally open. The register was taken. Then there was a last-minute check that everyone had their packed lunch, coat, beach towel, bucket and spade, and most importantly, had been to the toilet!

Best friends Caitlin, Fatima and Kieran, lined up at the front of the queue outside – they really wanted the back seat on the coach before anyone else could get it! They were even looking forward to the journey on the coach; the usual routines of comparing sandwiches, making faces and waving at people out the back window, or unzipping bags while people weren't looking... The girls also wanted to sing, though Kieran had no idea why. Then there were the dream pranks of putting a banana skin under one of the teacher's feet, so they'd slip, and (even harder to achieve) putting a frog in a teacher's bag!

West the coach went, zigging southwest from Kells to Mullingar in Co. Westmeath, then up northwest through Co. Longford and Co. Roscommon, until finally, nearly four hours later, they had arrived at Fallmore (Fál Mór), Co. Mayo. They had super fun on the journey of course (and there were a few short toilet-breaks on the way).

Everyone was glad to pile out of the coach. There was a strong breeze blowing in their faces from the Atlantic Ocean, but the sky was blue and no coats were needed. They walked up some stone steps until finally, they had arrived at St Darbiled's church ruins. They walked through the long grass that had grown up around the old building, then past some headstones of graves until they found a good spot to sit. It was a beautiful location, with the mountains in the background and the ocean to the other side. All were now looking forward to hearing the story of Darbiled and her church. The tour guide was called Brian, and he was likewise keen to start his story. And so he began.

'This is a story about a girl from Co. Meath, with unwavering willpower.' he said. 'Her father was a nobleman called Cormac. He was proud that he could trace his ancestry far, far back. He was son of Breech, son of Eochad, son to David, son of Fiach, ancestor of the royal Connacht dynasty of Uí Fhiachrach. Her brother was called Triallach and he became a church leader. And the medieval Book of Leinster says that her mother was called Cuman, daughter of Dallbhrónach. That means she came from a huge extended family through her mum. Cuman had either 20 or 47 saint sons and daughters! Some of Darbiled's siblings were her sister, St Moninne of Killeavy, Co. Armagh, and her brother, St Senán of Scattery Island, Co. Clare. Some of her cousins were St Brigid of Kildare and St Íte of Killeedy.

'Now, as you'll find happened to a lot of our Irish wonder women,' he continued, 'long ago arranged marriages were the norm, especially among nobility. However, Darbiled did not want to get married, even though her suitor was a prince! His actual job was that he was a chief in the army.'

Fatima and her family had come as refugees from a country where forced child marriages happened. So this issue was particularly relevant to Fatima (though forced and arranged marriages are different).

Brian continued, 'So, early one morning before anyone in her home was awake, Darbiled, with resolve and single-mindedness, set off all on her own! She was determined to get rid of her admirer. Miles and miles she travelled by donkey ('Asal' in Irish), as far west as she could go (actually, she was so stressed, that she veered off course from the setting sun in the west, so it was northwest she headed). Now, it took you children four hours to travel here by coach this morning. Imagine how long it took Darbiled on her donkey. On and on Darbiled went, right over to here, Fallmore, on this Mullet Peninsula, which we also call the Erris Peninsula. You can see, if she had travelled any further west in Ireland, she would have been in the Atlantic Ocean! Darbiled built a little church called Iris Cethig in what became the parish of Kilmore, and lived a very happy life.

'Until – can you children think what might have happened? – one day the prince appeared! As part of his plan to win her over, he told her that her eyes were most beautiful eyes he'd ever seen. Now, Darbiled wasn't accepting any of that flattery. She was furious! In her anger, Darbiled gouged out her beautiful eyes and threw them on the ground at the feet of the prince. He was so shocked he thought he was going to vomit! He headed back to Co. Meath as fast as he could, never to return.

'Now, there is a happier ending to the story. Where her eyes landed on the ground, a well sprang up. She washed the blood from her face with the fresh water and a miracle happened. Darbiled's sight returned! As it says in the Bible:

> *God is our refuge and strength, an ever-present help in trouble.*
> – Psalm 46:1, NIV

'Today in Fallmore, you can see this old, granite church ruin beside where we are standing,' Brian continued. 'It dates from the twelfth century, on the site of Darbiled's church, which she built perhaps in 585 AD. We also know from the Annals of Connacht that, in 585 AD, St Darbiled, accompanied by St Geidh from Inis Geidhe and St Muirdeach from Ballina, travelled to the Synod of Bishops in Ballysadare (in Co. Sligo), to meet with St Columba (or Colmcille in Irish). St Columba was a very famous monk who started lots of churches. Darbiled must have been a great church leader to be invited to such a gathering.

'Now, are any of you children up for an adventure? As you can see, there is only one small window left of the twelfth-century ruins of Darbiled's church beside us. It is on the east side of the church. If you can fit through, they say you'll never drown! In another version of the story, it is said that you will go straight to heaven if you go through it three times.' Brian spoke with lots of mystery in his voice, so no one was sure yet if they would fit through it!

'You can see the grave of Darbiled over there on the other side of the church. There are also some beautiful modern standing stones called 'Deirbhile's Twist' a few minutes' walk away, which your teachers are going to show you later. Darbiled's holy well is also here, just a short coach journey to the northwest. It is said to heal eye problems, of course. A pilgrimage takes place annually to the well on 15th August. There is also a second holy well at Doonfeeny in the adjoining barony of Tirawley. So kids, who knows what will happen if you wash your eyes in their waters?'

☞ *Can you guess what they all answered?*

❖ ❖ ❖

'Now kids,' said Brian, 'my story about Darbiled is over, but before I finish my talk, put your hand up if you noticed the headstones and crosses on graves that you walked past.' A lot of hands went up. Brian then explained, 'This cemetery holds the graves of nine men and boys who died in one of the most tragic events ever to befall this area...the Cleggan Bay Disaster, or "the drowning" as we call it around here. There is a memorial for the nine here, and for three others who died in another drowning, so twelve in total.'

Brian continued, 'Many years ago, on 28th October 1927, it was a fine clear day. The sea was as calm as a mirror of glass they said. All along the coast of the counties Mayo and Galway, the fishermen were at work, getting their boats and nets ready for setting out that evening. Huge shoals of mackerel were along the shores and they were looking forward to a fine catch. Off they all set in their currachs from various islands and villages on the mainland – Inishkea Islands, Inishbofin Island, Rossadilisk near Cleggan, and Lacken. Yet, even though they were only a short distance from shore, at about 7:30 p.m. a terrible storm began. They found out later that it was Force 10 on the Beaufort Scale. The waves were so churned up, the sea looked white. One man who survived said, "We were blown about like a feather in the wind." The storm lasted for about two hours. After 9:30 p.m., the people counted up everyone who had not returned home. Forty-five young men and teenagers from nearby were all drowned! One 14-year-old boy from Inishkea, Terry Reilly, is buried here with his father.' Brian finished: 'It was a really terrible tragedy.' With heads bowed, they all then said a short prayer for the fishermen and their families.

By now it was already lunchtime, so after Brian was finished the children got out their picnics and had their sandwiches by the church ruins. It was a great place to wonder about whether they could squeeze through the church window. Later Brian allowed everyone to see if they could indeed squeeze through that east window he had told them about. There was a stepping-stone below the window on the outside of the church, so that they could reach up to it. And, of course, being children, they all fit through! Brian had just been speaking with suspense to make his story better. Even their teachers, Mrs. Wilson and Mrs. Neeson, could do it. So everyone was very chuffed at fitting through!

Now they were free to have a play in the sand and paddle on the beach (though no swimming allowed). Lots of sandcastles were built with water bucketed from the sea for filling the moats! Their volunteer parents who had come with them were busy drying and shaking off the children's wet sandy feet before they could get back into their socks, trainers, sandals or shoes.

With a short four-minute walk to the east, they visited 'Deirbhile's Twist'. It was a sculpture created by the artist Michael Bulfin in 1993. He made it by raising granite boulders that were already on the site and placed them in an ascending spiral (in order of increasing height). They had fun counting the 22 stepping-stones leading up to it. It was nice to see it but not as good as hearing Darbiled's eye story.

Next, they all got into their coach again. They had all been looking forward to seeing St Deirbhile's holy well. It only took three minutes in the opposite direction to get there. You see, Caitlin had been given a new watch for her birthday, so was timing everything! The holy well had a large altar to the front of it with a cross on top. This was painted with white and a light blue colour. Like many holy wells, there was a statue of the Virgin Mary inside the altar. A wall surrounded it with some flowers in pots sitting on top of the wall. Someone had obviously been taking good care of it all. All the children had a very good look at the underground spring gushing out of the well. Most of them reached down to touch the water. It had surely taken on a deeper significance now that they knew Darbiled's story.

One of their teachers explained the well's Irish name, Tobar Naomh Deirbhile. Not everyone spoke Irish, you see. 'Tobar' is the word for 'well', and 'naomh' is the word for 'saint'. Then the other teacher explained that those visiting the well, especially on the pattern day of 15th August, walk around it nine times (three times on the knees and six times standing). While you do this, you recite the Rosary three times. Some of the children walked around the well nine times. Some did it just for fun, and some prayed at the same time. Others decided to just have a walk around before getting back into the coach or sit down on the wooden benches dotted further up the hillside. There were a few friendly cows on the other side of a barbed wire fence and some of the children, especially those who weren't from farms, wanted to pet them. Finally, the two teachers collected some of the well water to take home with them.

Then, back into the coach they all got. 'Bye, Darbiled!' called one of the girls. Up slightly north they went to Aughleam. In six minutes, they were there (Caitlin was still timing everything) and filed into the St Deirbhle heritage centre called Io-nad Deirbhile in Irish. It had a ten-foot stained-glass window that shows Darbiled and her little donkey, with nice flowers in glass at the bottom. This window is a replica of the window outline found in the old church ruins at Fallmore. It was very pretty and modern. Everyone gazed up and wished that they could actually meet Darbiled and her little donkey. As if reading their thoughts, one of the people who worked at the museum asked them all, 'Now children, if you could ask Darbiled just one question, what would it be?' Before you read on in the story, can *you* think of anything that *you* would like to ask Darbiled if you could meet her?

The children started asking their questions. 'How on earth did you get your eyes out?' called out one of the boys. Kieran had put him up to it, as he didn't want to get in trouble in case it was a bit too gory to ask. 'What did your little donkey eat all that way on the long journey from Co. Meath?' said Fatima. Caitlin said, 'I would ask Darbiled, did you know that God was going to heal your eyes? Did God tell you before you pulled them out that you'd get them back again?' Everyone was full of good questions. 'Would there have been lots of blood when her eyes came out?'; 'Did Darbiled feel like fainting when she saw the blood?'; 'Did Darbiled's mum and dad hear about what happened to her?'; 'Do we know anything more about her brother, Triallach?'

On and on, the class thought of great questions. The museum staff and their two teachers had an interesting time trying to answer as many questions as they could. Now that you've heard the children's questions, can you think of any others that you would ask Darbiled?

At the museum in Aughleam, they also learned lots of other things through the artefacts on display about what life was like in Co. Mayo in the past. One of the artefacts was a 'creel', a big square basket that was attached in pairs across a donkey's back. Creels were used to carry heavy loads of turf, seaweed and potatoes. Perhaps Darbiled's donkey had creels on him when he carried Darbiled (and maybe some of her possessions) all that long journey from Co. Meath to Co. Mayo!

Then it was time to head back home to Kells in Co. Meath. On the way home, their teachers set them this task below. Everyone got busy working on it. They were all actually glad to have some work to do!

Don't be bland, put the pen on hand!

Darbiled's name is spelt lots of ways, but it means 'daughter of the filí'. A filí was a poet. Write a poem about Darbiled or how you would feel about marrying someone you didn't want to! Your poem doesn't have to be an epic (a very long story poem). It could be a short limerick, haiku, or acrostic.

✤ ✤ ✤

From Meath to Mayo
Trundling along
My heart is grey, Oh
Lord hear my song!

From Meath to Mayo
I want to be free
From suitors and no say, Oh
I long for the sea!

From Meath to Mayo
West and west I go
On donkey day by day, Oh
Lord I trust you so!

❋ **Feast days:** 3rd August.

❋ **Other names:** Deirbhle, Dairbhile, Deirbhileadh, Dirbhileadh, Dervla, Dervila, Derbiled, Dervilla and Derrivla.

❋ According to the Hidden History of Holy Wells, there are 187 holy wells in Northern Ireland and 2,996 in the Republic of Ireland. However, for example in Northern Ireland, Dr. Celeste Ray has written that nearly a third of holy wells lack a documented name and only twelve are still in regular use.

❋ Forced marriages today are condemned by the United Nations. They are different from an arranged marriage. Forced child marriage is especially condemned.

❋ St Dairbhile's Church is designated a National Monument of Ireland.

❋ Although Darbiled was descended from a royal family in the province of Connacht, the tradition at the Saint Deirbhile Heritage Centre, Co. Mayo, is that she travelled from Co. Meath (in the province of Leinster).

Demon-slayer Dymphna

Once, long ago, there lived a beautiful teenage Irish princess called Dymphna. She was only fourteen years old at the beginning of our story. Let me tell you all about her and her family.

Her father, Damon, was a minor king of a small kingdom in Oriel (Airgíalla) in south Ulster (the province in the north of Ireland) and Co. Louth. He was a pagan, someone who followed the Druid religion, unlike her mother who was a Christian. Dymphna was also a Christian. Tragedy struck Dymphna's young life when her devoted mother died. It took an even darker, more tragic turn after that because, you see, her father loved her mother very dearly and his grief soon turned to madness! His counsellors advised him to remarry, so servants were sent out to search many countries for a potential wife. Yet, the only face that interested Damon was Dymphna's. Each day she grew more and more the image of her mother. Since she bore such a striking resemblance to her mother, Damon decided he wanted to marry Dymphna. Dymphna was horrified!

But Dymphna was a clever girl and she asked her father for forty days to consider his proposal, and sought wisdom from her old faithful Christian priest, Gerebern. His advice was that they flee as soon as possible to Europe's mainland. Off set Dymphna and Gerebern, her father's court jester, and his wife (they were all Christians). For what seemed like an age, they travelled over land and sea until, finally, in the spring they reached the city of Antwerp in Brussels. It was a huge port by the North Sea. But their presence there needed to be completely secret! Wanting greater seclusion, they all went further inland. Their boat zig-zagged up and up the tributaries, for miles and miles, up the River Scheldt, then the Rupel and then the Nete until finally they were happy that they were safe in the countryside of the Campine, far to the east. There they found a small hamlet called Geel. That region is full of forests, moors, wetlands and sandy heaths, so there were no big

89

cities. Surely, word would never reach her father that she had gone to what is now the country of Belgium? Surely, he'd also never know which water ways they had taken their boat up, even if he guessed the correct country? Surely, she was safe?

As soon as she got there, brave Dymphna immediately decided she would help those around her. The people of Geel were afraid of demons and ghosts, who they believed flew around on wild goats in the night to scare people! They were called 'the Buckriders'. They cast spells 'across houses, across gardens, across stakes, even across Cologne into the wine cellar'. Once a year, they would visit their master, the Devil! It might seem silly to our ears, but back then people believed the stories. Those stories of demons had the people completely demoralized; their morale and confidence had all but gone. Even today we know of such stories in Belgium. There was no way Dymphna would allow the villagers to suffer such worry. She told them the truth that these were just scary, made-up stories. As well as that, the Bible taught that Jesus released people from demons (or evil spirits), so Dymphna taught the people about Christianity and then prayed that those worried about demons would not feel oppressed any more.

Also, after seeing her father's problems with his mind, she decided to help those who had mental illnesses in Campine. For example, anyone with extreme sadness, worry and anxiety, or believing things that weren't real, she tried to help (there is more detailed information about mental illnesses later in the story). Dymphna taught the people with her knowledge of the Bible:

> *Humble yourselves, therefore, under God's mighty hand, that he may lift*
> *you up in due time. Cast all your anxiety on him because he cares for you.*
> – 1 Peter 5: 6-7, NIV

In the old Flemish language, Dymphna was soon called 'Een Lilie onder de Doornen', which meant 'a lily among thorns'. She was also known as the Lily of Éire (Ireland) due to her spotless virtue (her goodness and holiness).

Now, meanwhile in Oriel, Ulster, her father Damon became even more demented with anger. He ordered that Ireland and beyond be searched, high and low. He opened the royal treasury and offered a reward for information leading to the capture of poor Dymphna. He ordered that everyone at the Ulster ports be detained and questioned! Slowly but surely, he got the information that he was paying for and tracked their route until his fleet of ships was finally at Antwerp. Unaware of this, Dymphna and her servants used Irish money at the nearby market in Westerloo one day, not far from Geel. This left a huge clue that was discovered shortly after.

The dreaded day their small group had thought impossible had arrived. Damon and his men stood before Dymphna. With grand promises that seemed sensible to his pagan mind, he tried to convince Dymphna to return to Ireland with him. He reminded her that if she'd stayed with him, she would have inherited his kingdom when he died. But Dymphna was only concerned with the kingdom of God by looking after the ill and poor now. She didn't care about power over people or money.

He promised to build a fine temple of marble where she would be worshipped as a goddess. He would build a superb statue of her with gold and precious stones, and put it inside the temple. And if anyone didn't worship Dymphna, they would be severely punished. Well, being a good Christian who knew idolatry (worshipping idols) was wrong, that didn't persuade Dymphna either.

Old faithful and honest Gerbern spoke up to defend Dymphna, saying how wicked the King was. But immediately, full of rage, Damon ordered his men to behead him! Dymphna was filled with even more bravery and called her father a detestable tyrant. She said that she was prepared to accept whatever fate lay before her. Damon's men were reluctant to hurt Dymphna but, enraged and in a frenzy at what she had said, Damon pulled his own sword from his scabbard. With one deadly blow, he cut off his innocent daughter's head. Immediately, Dymphna was in heaven. She was only fifteen years old when she was martyred.

Today, St Dymphna is the patron saint of the whole Campine region. In 1349, a church honouring St Dymphna was built in Geel where she was buried. By 1480, so many pilgrims were coming from all over Europe, seeking treatment for the mentally ill, that townspeople began taking them into their own homes. They wanted to carry on Dymphna's good work. They called these ill people 'boarders'.

The father of the famous nineteenth-century painter, Vincent van Gogh, considered sending Vincent to Geel. Vincent, you see, struggled with severe depression. In just under ten years of his short life, Vincent painted many wonderful works of art (about 2,100 artworks, including around 860 oil paintings). Do you know of any of them? Perhaps you have seen his *Sunflowers* series or *The Starry Night* in school?

Despite his sadness, Vincent still had a favourite colour. Can you guess what it was (think about his paintings)? It seems to have been yellow! Do *you* have a favourite colour? Or one that makes you especially happy?

Now, I've mentioned examples of mental illness already, but you might like more information. What exactly are mental illnesses? Mental illnesses are types of illnesses in the mind (in the brain part of your head). Like all illnesses, you can see there are different kinds, and they are just as real. For example, being afraid to meet with others or go outside, extreme sadness, thoughts that life isn't worth living, extreme worry, extreme anxiety, believing things that aren't real, or seeing/hearing things that aren't real. You are right that it sounds very serious.

Just before Vincent van Gogh died, his last words were, 'The sadness will last forever.' *But* unlike long ago, there is now excellent medication for these serious illnesses. For example, there are many types of tablets and even painless injections for them that can work wonders! Talking about your problems can also give a lot of help too. A person who is trained to talk about mental health problems with you is called a counsellor. You could spend time doing things that make you happy. It is good to go outside to a forest, park or garden, taking time to be with nature. Exercise (sport, walking, swimming etc.), listening to music, getting enough sleep and relaxing are all important too. Everyone knows that you should try to eat a healthy, balanced diet with lots of fruit and vegetables. But did you know that certain foods, like bananas, nuts and chocolate (in small amounts) contain lots of 'happy hormones' that help your brain to work well?

If you think you are affected by any of these mental illnesses, it is extremely important that you speak to an adult. You could talk to a parent, your doctor, a nurse (especially if there's one in your school), or a teacher. All these people are there to help you, and they would be very upset if they knew you were suffering in silence!

In Geel at its peak in 1938, Belgium, there were 3,736 'boarders' (placed patients). Today, a modern psychiatric centre stands in place of the old infirmary and about 250 patients are still placed with townspeople.

Dymphna is very much still remembered today, especially in Belgium. In 1975, there was a Belgian stamp released that portrayed the beheading of St Dymphna. It shows her father Damon, with his sword raised, just about to cut off Dymphna's head!

In religious art, Dymphna is often portrayed wearing a crown, dressed in ermine fur and royal robes, holding a sword. Do you know what ermine is? Ermine is the white winter fur and black tail end of an animal called the stoat. It was worn in the past by royalty and high officials. Dymphna, after all, was an Irish princess. Sometimes her sword is shown pricking the neck of a demon (symbolising her title of Demon-slayer). Sometimes, she holds a white lily (representing her spotless virtue). Sometimes, she is shown holding a lamp with the devil chained at her feet. The lamp symbolises the light of the good news of Christianity that she brought to Belgium. Dymphna sure earned her title of 'Demon-slayer Dymphna'!

Let's do art!

TASK

Like Vincent van Gogh, draw or paint a picture (or pictures)
of something that makes you happy. Use lots of your
favourite colour!

DID YOU KNOW?

❋ **Feast day:** 15th May (main) & 11th April (St Dymphna & St Gerebern's arrival to Antwerp).

❋ **Feast day of St Gerebern:** 15th May. His relics were moved to Xanten in Germany (feast day: 20th July).

❋ **Other names:** Dympna

❋ There is a St Dymphna's Special School in Ballina, Co. Mayo.

❋ There is even a shrine dedicated to St Dymphna at St Mary's Catholic Church in Massillon, Ohio, US.

❋ The word 'martyr' comes from the Greek word for 'witness'. Dymphna became a martyr since she bore witness to her faith in God by refusing to marry her father.

Formidable Faber

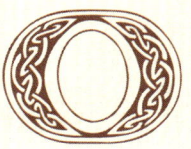nce upon a time, in the days when St Patrick was an old man, there lived a young girl called Faber (or Fedbair). Her home was in Killydrum townland in Boho (pronounced 'Boh'), in Co. Fermanagh. That is all in Ulster (the province in the north of Ireland). Boho is a mountainous area about 7 miles (11.27 km) southwest of the town of Enniskillen. According to the Tract on the Mothers of the Saints, Faber's father was called Dallbhrónach and he was a king. She was part of a very large extended family. She had at least six sisters: Cuman (mum of either 20 or 47 children!), Broicseach (Brigid of Kildare's mum), Caiomheall, Fuinche (not the Fanchea in this book), Feidhealm (Íte's mum) and Bhróg.

Like all the people in the Boho area, Faber's family followed the religion of the druids. Often, they gathered at the sacred Refad stones to worship the pre-Christian gods of sun, sky, rivers and trees. Faber's father regularly told her the story of how his ancestors were buried at the great tomb monument in Aughnaglack, some distance to the south of her home.

Then one day, they heard the great St Patrick preaching. Faber's niece, who would become the famous Brigid of Kildare, had met him too and was following the new faith of Christianity. The family were so impressed with the teaching about Jesus that they were baptised and became Christians. Some of their friends and neighbours, who still followed the teaching of the druids, were angry with them and stopped being their friends.

Faber wanted to become a nun, so she wrote down everything on Christian teachings that she heard into books. Then she thought about where she would build her church.

To quote from Boho Heritage Organisation's heritage picture map, 'Boho gets its name from the Irish word 'botha', meaning 'huts'. It is an area of outstanding natural beauty, with famous caves, scenic walks and the largest pothole in Ireland! To say it is beautiful would be an understatement, and we shall mention some of the famous sights. Faber wanted an outstanding inspirational location. After all, the pagan druids before the days of Christianity had left the ruins of an amphitheatre, which they had used for their meetings. So, Faber wanted an equally splendid location.

There were so many interesting sites in Boho. As well as the hills, forests and loughs, there was the Bobo cave system. That would have been interesting but a bit dark, she thought. Noon's Hole or 'Sumera' meant 'abyss'. It is the deepest pothole in Ireland. It goes right down into the ground for 250 feet (76.2 metres). But again, that was too dark too. There were tombs, but she thought that they were probably associated with burial sites too much, as from even more ancient times burials took place at those sites. Her faith was anything but dead! There were lovely waterfalls, but Pollagallum waterfall, for example, is beside one of the many caves in the area, so it wasn't possible to be really close to it. Also, many of the local people were scared of the caves. The old religious thoughts linked them with fairies and other such folks of the Otherworld, who would entice you down into the earth with their music, never to see light of day again. No, she wanted a site that linked her to the past but that was also a beautiful inspiration.

She settled in the end near the beautiful Refad stones. The Refad stones are six ancient, large stones on the side of a hill that are 4,000-5,000 years old. Five of them are decorated in amazing cup and ring markings. Being beside such an ancient site might remind people, she thought, that God is even older; He is ever-lasting! It would also make a point to her neighbours, who were still druids, that Christianity was triumphing over paganism. It was also right beside a well, so there would be water to drink too.

Faber walked all over the area telling her message. Her sister, Bhróg, had become a nun as well and she helped her. Faber walked the Barrs (the high ground), she walked down by the Bottoms, along the banks of the winding Sillees River, up Belmore Mountain to the southeast, and around Ora bog. She talked to the people and told them all that she had learned about Jesus. Some people listened to her and became Christians; others laughed, shouted at her and even threw stones at her! Now, she started to build a wooden church.

There is a story of how, after Faber had started building, she came back the next morning to see what she'd built the day before, only to find it had been

95

knocked down! Everyone said it was one of the invisible beings, a fairy, banshee or changeling, one of the myriad folklore beings that were spoken of so much in that part of Fermanagh in pagan times. Even today, locals refer to the 'Faerie Circle', which lies on the hill above where Faber tried to build her church.

However, Faber prayed and felt that there was a safer, better place to build her church. Before we continue, there is one interesting fact to know about Faber, and that is that she had a lovely pet deer. It was a young male.

Now, Faber prayed about her church location problem and her little deer obviously knew what God was saying too, for it motioned for Faber to follow her. Her deer carried her bag of books with her notes from St Mo Laisse and St Ninnidh (both famous local monks) down to Monea, off to the northeast of Boho. But they had to cross the Sillees River at some point. Now, everyone in old Ireland knew that the troublesome 'little people' as they were called often lived in rivers. One in particular, called a 'síofra' ('water-sprite'), lived in the Sillees. It was a type of elfish water-sprite. When Faber's deer stepped into the water, what do you think happened? Of course, the little deer was made to trip! The bag of books fell off his young horns and Faber's holy books were dropped into the river! You see, the síofra didn't want Christianity to be spread in the area. It had put an enchantment ('siabhair' in Irish) upon the water in the river.

Well, Faber was rightly livid with anger and cursed the river. She said the Sillees would be bad for fishing (it says in the Irish that the fish would die) and good for drowning (humans would die too)! It sounds like a very serious punishment, but it was absolutely essential that she tell everyone the good news from her holy books. Faber was fearsome. She couldn't be a wilting violet starting a church!

In another more well-known version of the story, Faber was on her way one lovely sunny day to meet Baron O'Fialain at his castle in the townland of Aghamore. She asked him for some food for the local poor. For the Bible taught that we should treat others as we'd like to be treated, and to especially look after the poor:

> *Whoever is kind to the poor lends to the Lord,*
> *and he will reward them for what they have done.*
> – Proverbs 19:17, NIV

But Baron O'Fialain, who was head druid and didn't follow Christian teaching, did not take kindly to Faber's request. O'Fialain and two big angry hounds came out of the castle door as he cried, 'Get away from my house, leave my people alone! Stop leading the people astray with your false God!' He told his hounds to chase Faber and her deer, so the hunting dogs went after Faber's beloved pet deer. To escape, the deer jumped into the Sillees River and, in the process, ruined her books! Faber fell to her knees. She placed *another* curse on the river that it would run up-hill and *backwards*. 'Running against the height until judgement day', is the literal translation from Irish. Beforehand, the Sillees River ran from Boho towards the sea! The story goes that 'the river writhed and recoiled' and now it goes towards Upper Lough Erne rather than the sea.

It is said that if you look closely at the way the river goes today you can still see some of the old routes that have dried up or formed oxbow-like depressions in the ground. You see, when a slow river flows, it pushes out the water to the edges of the banks and that is how meanders are formed. Sometimes the meanders become so pronounced (so bendy) that the bends break off and form little lakes to the sides of the river. These little lakes are called ox-bow lakes. Sometimes over a long time, these dry out to form dry impressions that leave a ghostly imprint of a river path that once was. Some people say that a ghost imprint of the old riverbed can still be seen in Co. Fermanagh.

Another great story about Faber is that she went back to Baron O'Fialain's castle to curse it too. She needed to teach that Baron a lesson! She prayed so hard that the ground opened up and swallowed his castle! She was trying to build a home for God's people after all, so she would take his home away from him. It sunk down in so deep that the grass closed over it and no one in the area could see where the castle used to be. However, locals know the area where it was. It is called Poll More (Poll Mór), and it is just a short distance south of Faber's church and well.

After that, Faber and her deer, safely retrieved from the river, walked to Monea. There she built a church beside another well in Killyveigh and lived in Monea for many years. Her little deer grew up to become a huge stag with impressive antlers. He would go off without Faber to join herds of other deer each mating season (the 'rut'). But he would come back every so often to visit Faber.

Another story about Faber tells that one Friday she was invited to Lough Melvin, for a feast with Co. Fermanagh noblemen. Whatever happened, Faber was distracted and didn't realise that they had set down chicken in front of her to eat. They had done it on purpose! The noblemen knew that at that time Christians were not allowed to eat any meat on Fridays, although they were permitted to eat fish. They thought it would be a great joke. But just as Faber was about to bite into the chicken, she realised what it was! She cursed it and it turned into fish. But not cooked fish. Living fish appeared, then jumped into Lough Melvin! That is how the 'Gillaroo' lives in Lough Melvin, its only home.

When she was an old lady, Faber returned to see Killydrum and Boho. Today there exists the remains of a high cross there, which is dated to the tenth century. If you would like to see it, it is at the local Catholic Sacred Heart Church. There is also a holy well and bullaun stone there (in a field owned by Brian Maguire) both named for St Faber. Faber's picture is also in the stained-glass windows of the churches in Boho and Monea.

Your own creation Story

It is said that Faber was responsible for the Gillaroo fish.
Write your own creation story about how a new species of
animal was made!

DID YOU KNOW?

❀ **Feast days:** 6th November, & 7th July (in Oughteragh parish, Co. Leitrim).

❀ **Other names:** Fedbair, Feadhbhair, Fionnbharr and Fiadhabhair.

❀ People have traditionally come from far and wide to take home the limestone clay soil from Boho churchyard, as it has been said to have healing properties. In 2018, the BBC news reported it contains a unique strain of streptomyces, a microorganism used to produce antibiotics. It was found to kill the top three organisms that cause disease identified by the World Health Organisation (WHO) as a major threat to human health!

❀ There are five species of deer in Ireland today (red, fallow, sika, Reeve's muntjac and roe), though the Reeve's muntjac is in very small numbers. Faber's pet deer would have been a red deer ('Fia Rua' in Irish). The red deer is Ireland's largest land mammal and is the only species of deer that is native to Ireland.

Fantastic Fanchea

Fanchea (or Fuinche), like so many of our wonder women, was born into a noble family. Her father was called Connall Dearg ('Connall the Red'), and he was a prince of the old kingdom of Oriel (Airgíalla) in south Ulster. She was born at a place called Rathmore, near Clogher, one of the two main towns in that kingdom. That is in present day Co. Tyrone. Her mother was called Briga, or Aibfinn. We know that Fanchea had at least one brother, Énda, and three sisters, Caírech, Lochina and Darenia. Fanchea was known for her extraordinary beauty. She had stunning, raven-black locks of long hair. When she was born, her parents chose her name because of her distinctive hair colour. Fanchea (or Fuinche) means either 'scald-crow' or 'black fox'.

But, as we shall see, her remarkable virtues made her even more admirable than her beautiful looks did! Fanchea was a girl whose personality could be described with four fantastic P's. Prophetic, persuasive, persistent and powerful.

Like some of the prophets in the Bible, you will see that Fanchea sometimes did strange things to communicate her point. She wanted to make sure that her preaching really sunk in. These 'prophetic' things are dotted throughout her story.

Now, it is said that King Óengus mac Nad Froích of Cashel, in Co. Tipperary, wished to marry Fanchea. But even though we know that he was the first Christian King of Munster (and a very devout Christian), Fanchea resolved to become a nun! The story goes that, to escape being married, Fanchea went to Co. Fermanagh. There she dived into Lough Erne and then the River Shannon, and swam all the way to Inchcleraun, an island on Lough Ree! Lough Ree was halfway down Ireland, in Co. Longford – she must have been a super swimmer! It was a distance of approximately 76 miles (122 km). When Fanchea arrived there at Díarmait the Just's church, she was covered in shells and slime from the water. That is how she got

101

her nickname in Irish, Fuinche 'garb', or 'gharbh', which means 'rough', as she was rough with slime and shells all over her. Fanchea then persuaded King Óengus to marry her sister Darenia, which he did!

So Fanchea got what she wanted (not to marry, and to become a nun). She was persuasive and persistent. She then decided to start her convent in the centre of Co. Fermanagh, not that far from home. It was in Lisgoole townland within what is Rossorry (Ross Airthir) parish. She had a beautiful view out over the banks of Lough Erne. Fanchea was a fabulous leader and greatly respected, so many other young girls from royal homes came to be her disciples at Rossorry.

When her father died, her brother Énda succeeded as chieftain. And as chieftain's often had to do, he was at a battle one day against a neighbouring clan. As his men were coming home, triumphant from winning, they were singing. Fanchea was not impressed, and said to her nuns, 'Know you, my sisters, this dreadful singing is not pleasing to Christ!' Fanchea knew that her brother's heart was not to be a warrior fighting and not to kill in battle, so she told him so. But Énda argued that he was doing what was expected of him, like their father; Fanchea warned that their father was paying for the blood he had shed in the afterlife. Fanchea, as it were, started to sow the seeds of fear of God into her brother.

Énda continued to think about the things Fanchea had said to him about paying for sins after death. He said to her that he'd think about it, and asked in the meantime for a wife from one of her nuns. Now, a nun wasn't supposed to marry, but Fanchea gave it some thought. So, she decided to ask one of her nuns and, sure enough, she said yes, she'd marry Énda. Now, the story takes a strange turn, for shortly after Fanchea told the nun to lie down on her bed, she died (she went straight to heaven though of course)! Fanchea then brought Énda in to see her. He was struck with horror! Fanchea preached to him about what hell was like and what heaven was like, until young Énda, struck by the reality of death, burst into tears. Énda was ready to become a monk and received the tonsure.

Some of Énda's warriors were very unhappy at his decision and tried to get him back into his old ways. They came for him one day, but Fanchea knew about it. She prayed and their feet became stuck to the ground until they froze like statues! Again, this was another prophetic act that communicated that whoever wanted the 'things of the earth' should find themselves literally stuck to it.

Fanchea agreed with this Bible teaching:

> *Set your minds on things above, not on earthly things.*
> – Colossians 3:2, NIV

☞ ***Can you think of any examples of this?***

The next earth that Énda saw was the earth around Fanchea's convent. He put himself to good use, digging up deep trenches around it and weeding up all the thistles. Thanks to Fanchea's good teaching, the day came for Énda to set off. He went to Killanny (or Killaine, 'Cill Éanna') in Co. Louth, which is named after him. Some think he went there to start another convert for Fanchea. But another test of Énda's character happened to him one day there (when Fanchea was present). Some robbers came and their whole group set after them. Énda was just about to hit one of them when Fanchea warned him to touch his head. Of course, feeling his shaved head (as he had been tonsured), he remembered his vows and that he had chosen a way of peace as a monk.

Fanchea always thought about what was best for her brother and she felt that he would benefit from some time studying in Britain, so off he went. He stayed at a monastery called Rosnat (of uncertain location) under Abbot Mansenus. Sometime later, Fanchea entertained some visitors who had come from Rome (in present day Italy) to Ireland. They told her about a certain Irish monk called Énda and immediately Fanchea knew that it was her brother they were talking about! So she decided to pay him a visit in Britain with three of her nuns. When they arrived, Fanchea gave him some advice that would be another turning point in his life: she advised him to return to Ireland and go to the Aran Islands in Galway Bay. There, one day, Énda would become a great teacher of many, many students. Énda would most probably never have become the great spiritual leader that he did without Fanchea.

Later on, Fanchea visited Énda on Inishmore (Inis Mór), the largest of the Aran Islands. She was really pleased by the praying, fasting, and all their hard manual labour. There was also the beautiful copying of Latin gospels. When they were on their way home, Fanchea wouldn't allow Énda to ask some of his monks to row them across to the mainland in a currach. It is said that Fanchea was guided by angels, and so she said, 'We will trust to God for passage!' At the shore, she made the sign of the cross on the water and spread her cloak on it. At once her cloak became like a hard board! Fanchea and her nuns stood at each of the four corners and they sailed gently over the bay, even though the waters were rough. Galway Bay, after all, is beside the wild Atlantic Ocean. Fanchea was indeed a powerful woman of God! Her life was like an amazing fairy-tale at times.

It is said that Fanchea went to Rome on pilgrimage, and that she died on the return journey. Then the story continues that, with this news of her passing, there was a big argument between two different districts over where she would be buried! The people of Leinster fought with those of Meath for her body. Eventually, Fanchea's body was put into a cart drawn by two oxen and it was decided to let God decide which direction the oxen pulled it in. Now, the people of Leinster thought the oxen were bringing it to Barrigh, but some kind of illusion was happening as, in reality, the oxen and cart went to Killaine monastery, near Sliabh Breagh. It is not exactly clear where this Killaine was, but it was probably the Killaine or Killanny (Cill Éanna), in Co. Louth (which was said to have been founded by St Énda for St Fanchea). This is just a short distance north of the Co. Meath border.

So, what happened to Fanchea's convent at Lisgoole, Rossorry parish, Co. Fermanagh? Well, it later became a monastery for the Augustinians, and then the Franciscans. The Franciscans crossed a ford on the Sillees River to take care of local people in St Fanchea's Church. The name St Fanchea is still part of the full title for Rossorry Parish Church (the Church of Ireland).

☞ *Which part of Fanchea's prophetic, persuasive, persistent and powerful personality did you enjoy the most?*

How would you picture them?

~~~~~~~~~~~~~~~~~~ TASK ~~~~~~~~~~~~~~~~~~

Draw two pictures. One of Fanchea and her three nuns
sailing across Galway Bay on her cloak, and the other of
Fanchea covered with green slime and shells after she
swam down the River Shannon. Remember to colour
Fanchea's hair black!

~~~~~~~~~~~~~~~~ DID YOU KNOW? ~~~~~~~~~~~~~~~~

❀ **Feast days:** 1ˢᵗ January, & 29ᵗʰ March (Church of Ireland).

❀ **Other names:** Fuinche, Fainche, Fuinchea, Fainc, Funchea and Faine.

❀ There are *twelve* saints called Fanchea (or Fuinche).

❀ As well as Rossorry, Fanchea is also linked with Lough Ree (Loch Rí) on the River Shannon, Killanny (Cill Éanna), Co. Louth, and two places that have not been located: Tech Fainche and Cell Fainche ('house of Fanchea' and 'church of Fanchea').

❀ Fanchea is supposed to have had a bell that was rung against sinners.

❀ There is a St Fanchea's College in Enniskillen.

❀ Fanchea's sister, Caírech Dergain, is patroness of Cloonburren (Cluain Boirenn), Co. Roscommon. She was a nun there. The Dergain after her name has to do with a story where she blushed at an accusation made against Énda! (Feast day: 9ᵗʰ February). All of Fanchea's sisters are remembered as saints.

God-fearing Gobnait

Buzz, *buzz*, went a busy bee ('beach' in Irish). It was the month of June and a girl called Gobnait had wandered down to the beach and sea cliffs near her home. She lived in Co. Clare right beside the Atlantic Ocean, which stretches all the way down the west coast of Ireland. Co. Clare is in the southwest of Ireland (in the province of Munster). The female worker bees were feeding from the flowers, eating the nectar and pollen. They were so engaged with the centres of the flowers that they looked as if they were stuck inside! They especially liked the clumps of eye-catching 'sea pink' (or 'thrift') that grew in the nooks and crannies of the rocks near Gobnait's home.

One important thing to know about Gobanit was that she had always loved bees. She liked the beautiful butterflies that were there too, but she liked the bees even more – they were so extremely interesting! She had loved learning from her grandfather about what exactly the bees were doing to the pink flowers, and about how honey was made in their hives. Gobnait's grandfather had some beehives in hollow tree trunks. Since Gobnait was born to a wealthy aristocratic noble family, they could afford to eat honey on their bread. It was the only source of sweetness before sugar arrived in Ireland. Gobnait's grandfather also made mead to drink. It was an alcoholic drink made from honey, which was very popular with richer people. Her family also made candles from the beeswax that they scraped out of the hives. Beeswax candles burnt well and smelt nice. They didn't have to reply on cheaper tallow candles made from animal fat, which stunk the house out with their smoky, awful smell.

But today by the Ocean, as had been the case for several weeks, Gobnait was a girl full of sad thoughts. She wanted to be alone. She wandered if the bees ever got unhappy too. She decided that they were probably always happy, as they were much

106

too busy to be sad, and they weren't people after all. You see, Gobnait's grandparents had both died a few months ago in the springtime. That was one reason why she was unhappy. In Irish folklore, the soul of a person left as a bee or a butterfly when they died, so that was one reason why Gobnait was in deep contemplation with the bees that fine early summer day. For the last few weeks, she had been coming down to see the bees at the coast, keeping the Irish tradition of 'telling the bees'. You see, it was believed that if you didn't tell the bees of a wedding, a birth or a death, they would take offence and leave! And Gobnait didn't want her friends, the bees, to leave. So she told them all about how she missed her granny and granda.

Another reason Gobnait was sad was that there were lots of arguments in Gobnait's family. Gobnait's father was a prince. However, even though she was born into nobility, Gobnait didn't get any special treatment. Her family were always fighting among themselves.

Another thing to know about Gobnait was that she loved God, not just buzzy bees! Gobnait was also described as a God-fearing girl. Now, that doesn't mean that she was scared of God. No, it means she rightly respected Him. And so, on this particular day in June, Gobnait wandered over to one of the few wind-blown trees overlooking the waves below. She started to talk to the bees and God:

> *Little bee, little bee, can you see me,*
> *Sitting all alone, under this tree?*
> *Should I go off and sail to the sea,*
> *To escape all the quarrels and fights around me?*
>
> *What is the way to be happy each day?*
> *I follow God's way, so Lord, have Your say.*
> *I believe in Your power, Your strength, and Your might,*
> *I know You have a plan, so what is right in Your sight?*
>
> *Out in the sunshine, the bees have their work,*
> *And so I need mine, so I don't go berserk!*
> *I'm old enough to leave home, to go on the run,*
> *I'm so glum so I'll roam, for a life that is fun!*

Inside I'm sad and every day I grieve,
Little bee, and dear God, I think I should leave.
As honey is sweet and a real tasty treat,
I'll meet some kind Christians to learn from and greet!

And so, Gobnait, tearful and mournful, who also couldn't get any peace at home, decided to flee from her parents. She had heard of St Énda (St Fanchea's brother), a very famous monk. So, off she decided to travel to Inisheer (Inis Oírr), the smallest of the Aran Islands in Galway Bay. There, kind St Énda warmly welcomed her to study, and she learned about the Bible – and some more about bees!

Gobnait was very special at Inisheer, as she was the only female. She had her own little beehive hut ('clochán' in Irish), on the north side of the island near the seashore. She had no thoughts of leaving there, until one day an angel appeared to her! The angel said that the island with Énda was 'not the place of her resurrection' (the final place where she would die and be buried). Then the angel said that she should look for a place where she would find nine white deer grazing. Gobnait thought that that was all quite unusual, but it was definitely an angel who appeared to her, and it seemed very straightforward to find nine white deer. And, after all, she had begun her fun adventures listening to God, so she would continue listening to God's instructions – especially since an angel was involved! She did wonder, would there be any beehives where she found the nine white deer?

But where to look? Gobnait had an older brother called Abbán who had also left home. He was just one of her many brothers and sisters (who all became Christian leaders), but she had been especially close to Abbán. He had started a whole string of monasteries, so she thought she'd go in the direction of the last place she had heard he was at, somewhere in the south. It took some time of meandering through the counties of Limerick, Kerry and Waterford... Many of the places along the route of her journey even today carry her name or are devoted to Gobnait, like Dunquin (Dún Chaoin) and Milltown in Co. Kerry. Also, there are six places called Kilgobnet (Cill Ghobnait), one each in Co. Limerick, Co. Waterford, Co. Kerry, and three in Co. Cork! So by now, Gobnait had arrived into Co. Cork.

At various stages of her travels, she of course met deer. There were many of them back then, as there were so many more forests for them to live in. Each time she saw white deer, Gobnait counted them. She saw three at Clondrohid (Cluain Droichead) and six at Ballymakeera (Baile Mhic Íre), both in Co. Cork, but not exactly nine.

It was not enough. When she was down in Co. Cork, she had heard a rumour that her brother Abbán was in the area, so she carried on searching for the deer there. She had just crossed the Sullane river, a few miles west of Macroom, when suddenly she saw lots of deer...and they were all white! She started to count:

'One, two, three,
Oh my, let me see...
Can there be more?
Yes, there's four!
Four, five, six...
Are my eyes playing tricks?
Seven, eight, nine...
Yes! This is the sign!'

She had seen *nine* white deer by a well in the woods of Co. Cork. This must be the place, she thought. And then, who do you think appeared? Her brother!

Not long after that, Gobnait asked the local chieftain of that area (Muskerry) for land to build a church, and he agreed. It is thought that the chieftain was from the O'Herlihy family. Gobnait didn't ask for really good land; she had her church built on a rocky hillside near the river, looking towards the Derrynasaggart hills. Soon that place became known as Ballyvourney (Baile Bhúirne), which means 'town of the beloved'. You see, Gobnait soon became that 'beloved' as she was so loved by the local people.

As soon as Gobnait arrived at Ballyvourney, she set about beekeeping. She looked after the other nuns as well who soon came to stay with her, and she knew how to use honey for healing. There is at least one story of how she healed one of her nuns with honey.

As well as being God-fearing, Gobnait was also known for her goodness and kindness, especially to the poor. In the *Martyrology of Óengus*, Gobnait is described as having 'pure goodness', and 'as to God's love was opulent'. 'Opulent' implies that she was extremely wealthy, extravagant or luxurious about showing God's love. That brings to mind another story, which happened when Gobnait was a young girl living in Co. Clare. One day, she decided to take some meat to the local poor people. They couldn't afford fine food like meat as her noble family could. But on the way, she bumped into her father, who was not impressed and wanted to see exactly what she was carrying off to the local people. So she was forced to let her father see inside her basket! But when he looked in, what do you think he saw? The basket was now full of flowers. The meat had miraculously changed!

Since Gobnait loved bees and honey, she often used this Bible verse when she was teaching people about being kind and good:

> *Kind words are like honey – sweet to the soul and healthy for the body.*
> – Proverbs 16:24, NLT

☞ *Do you understand what it is saying? And do you like the taste of honey? Perhaps you've never tried it. Maybe someone (a teacher, church leader or parent etc.) could give you some to taste?*

❖ ❖ ❖

Now, God-fearing Gobnait didn't just rightly respect and love God, she also put the 'fear of God' into others! And Gobnait's bees weren't just very useful honey- and wax-making bees – they were also super-hero bees! There are super stories about them. On one occasion, invaders from the O'Donoghues of the Glens tried to carry away Gobnait's cattle. At this, her convent would have been left without milk from those cows! So Gobnait let loose the bees from her hives and they attacked the invaders. Off the O'Donoghues fled! As you've learnt, the early Irish believed that a bee carried the soul of a person, so that might be reason for added fear. And they also believed the soul could leave as a butterfly – but that would not have been anywhere near as scary.

In a different version of this story, the beehive turned into a bronze helmet and the bees turned into soldiers. The O'Herlihy family are said to have handed down the helmet through generations as a great source of protection. Legend says that it's now lost somewhere in Co. Kerry! Another version of the story has the beehive turning into a bell, which then became 'Gobnait's bell'.

God used Gobnait to perform other miracles too. One time, she kept the plague away from Ballyvourney by drawing a line along the eastern borders of the area with her stick, and the plague never crossed that line!

In another story, foreigners became intent on building a castle in Ballyvourney, but the local people didn't want it. Every night after the builders had left, Gobnait knocked down what they had built by throwing her bell at the castle (in another version, it is said that it was a stone ball, which is 'bulla' in Irish). Eventually those castle builders gave up. Gobnait never did stop having fun!

After this, the stone was often borrowed by people who wanted to cure themselves or their animals of illness. A woman from Macroom borrowed it to cure her cattle, but instead of returning it immediately she kept it for three nights. Strange loud noises started coming from the room where she had kept it. Absolutely terrified, that woman returned it on the fourth day. After that, the ball became mysteriously lodged in its present position at Gobnait's convent. Nowadays, pilgrims stop at the bulla and make the sign of the cross on it and three times on themselves. A ribbon or a handkerchief is then rubbed on the stone, which is taken home to prevent or cure illness.

Another tradition on her pattern day is that a thirteenth-century wooden statue of Gobnait is brought out for people to 'measure' the statue, with a ribbon around its neck, waist and feet. Again, it is then brought home to prevent or cure illness.

On pattern days, pilgrims walk 'rounds' ('turas' in Irish) around ten stations at Ballyvourney in a clockwise direction. And if you went there, do you think you'd see any deer? Well, there are metal deer on the church gates, but as well as that, it is said that even today a white male, a stag, can sometimes be seen at the holy well there.

Would you like to visit a beehive hut ('clochán' in Irish)? Well, if you would like to see Gobnait's beehive hut, there are the remains of one where she stayed on Inisheer, Co. Galway. It might be the actual one that Gobnait lived in! It is beside the later eleventh-century ruins of an oratory called St Gobnet's Church, which is a National Monument now.

As well as being the patron saint of bees, Gobnait is the patron of ironworkers/metalsmiths. 'Gobha' in Irish means 'smith'. Indeed, archaeologists did excavations at her church in Ballyvourney and found evidence of ironworking on the site. Gobnait truly was a woman way ahead of her time.

But Gobnait still remains most famous for her bees! If you visit Ballyvourney there is a statue of her there with large bees at the bottom of it, sculpted by Séamus Murphy and erected in 1951. There is also a famous stained-glass window in University College Cork of Gobnait and her bees driving off the thieves who tried to steal her cattle. It was designed by Harry Clarke in 1915. There is also a more recent, beautiful stained-glass window of Gobnait with her bees, designed by Joy McAllen in Dungarvan, Co. Waterford.

'Bee nice' like Gobnait

'Bee friendly' ideas! Plant flowers that bees especially like, such
as lavender and sunflowers, or leave a section of your garden
wild so dandelions can grow (they provide essential bee food).
For more of a challenge, build a 'bee hotel' for solitary bees!

DID YOU KNOW?

❁ **Feast day:** 11th February.

❁ **Other names:** Gobnaid, Gobnad, Abigail and Deborah.

❁ In old Brehon law, they wrote the bee-judgements ('bechbretha') in the seventh century. These covered all sorts of issues to do with bees. For example, what to do if bees trespassed, how to decide who owned bees, how to punish bee or honey theft, and how much honey a beekeeper should offer their neighbours. It is always important to have good manners!

❁ In modern Ireland, there are well over 2,000 beekeepers with 22,000 colonies of honeybees!

❁ In a Co. Kerry version of the story, Gobnait's father was a pirate who came ashore at Ventry (Fionntraigh) in Co. Kerry. However, there's not much evidence for this version.

❁ Some deer are white due to 'leucism', which causes the hair and skin to lose their natural colour. White deer were considered to be messengers from the Otherworld in some Celtic myths. The white deer that Gobnait saw would have actually been the red deer species with leucism.

❁ Bees taste not only with their tongue, jaws and antennae, but with their front feet! They beat their wings approximately 11,400 times every minute – that is what makes the buzzing sound. As well as making honey and wax, bees pollinate our crops.

113

Grimonia to Gaul

LA CAPELLE, FRANCE ❧ 4ᵀᴴ CENTURY

It was late one stormy September night in the middle of the English Channel (or 'la Manche', as it is called in French), when a young princess called Grimonia and her female companion, a girl called Proof, were fleeing their home in Ireland. They were sailing towards Gaul (as France was called then), but as they entered the 'channel' of sea between England and France, the wind picked up. The air whistled loudly and the waves whirled higher and higher. Their little ship was buffeted more and more by the huge waves breaking down upon it, until it was no longer a breeze blowing but a real winter's wind! White foam flew against the boat, sending a bitter chill to Grimonia and Proof's bodies. And yet, the cold was the least of their worries, as waves now chased across the sea towards them. Seagulls circled the mast, shrieking as if they were warning of worse to come. The sailors ran around the deck to look after the ship's sails. The captain at the tiller was trying to steer his ship as best he could. It wasn't long before the superstitious sailors wanted to know from the girls why they were travelling to Gaul, and whether they were the real cause of the storm!

Grimonia, being the princess and an honest girl, told the men her sad story. For indeed, she felt that perhaps she was to blame for the awful tempest which now engulfed them. Poor Proof was just her companion on this journey. Despite the roar of thunder and lightning now zipping across the sky, Grimonia began at the beginning.

Grimonia explained that her father was a pagan king in Ireland, deeply devoted to the old druid gods. But at age 12, she had made the decision to follow the new religion of Christianity. She was baptised and taught about the faith without the knowledge of her parents. Immediately, the sailors knew there was a strong chance the sea gods were taking vengeance on Grimonia and hence she was to blame for their current predicament in the storm!

But Grimonia begged them to let her finish her story. 'When I was older,' she said, 'my father, the King, organised for me to marry a rich nobleman. But when it came to the morning of the wedding ceremony, I slipped out from the palace as quietly as I could and hid! Everyone was looking for me but I'm afraid I hadn't chosen a good hiding place, for I was found soon after.' One of the sailors had decided he really wanted to hear Grimonia's story. He asked her, 'So what happened next? Did you have to get married? Did your god help you back then?' Grimonia winced and replied, 'Well actually, things got worse. But please let me finish my story. My father had me locked in prison!'

'What!' said the sailors, as more had now joined to listen. 'Well,' said Grimonia, 'I want you to know that my God, the real God, answers prayers. I think my father was planning on keeping me in prison until I changed my mind and would agree to marry the nobleman, but for many years now, I have decided to be a nun and not marry.'

Grimonia continued, 'In prison, I prayed and fasted for days. Then, all of a sudden, one night I saw a bright light and saw an angel standing near me. The angel was a being from heaven, sent from my God, and was so beautiful! I heard a crack and looked towards the prison doors. Right in front of me, the padlock crumbled into nothing and fell off. I could see it happen because of the light coming from the angel. The angel said, "Get up Grimonia, the doors of your cell are open, go out and head out to the sea!" With that, the angel shone a bright light that guided me through the dark prison to the way out. And as quickly as the angel had appeared, it disappeared. I was so shocked that I thought for a second I had just had a vision, but I was standing out in the open with the moonlight shining over my head.

'That's when I snuck into Proof's home and asked her if she wanted to join me. Proof's parents are staunch pagans too and wanted her to marry a pagan man. We had a little money to pay for passage on a ship, so made our way to the sea as fast as we could. Please, help us get to Gaul! We are both in great danger!'

The sailors were markedly changed as soon as Grimonia mentioned her story about the angel opening the prison cell doors for her. As the sea grew wilder and angrier, the men knelt down, despite the raging weather around them. They asked Grimonia how they too could follow this God of hers. Grimonia gladly shared her faith and prayed with them. Soon, there was a whole ship-load of new believers sailing to Gaul! Next, fearing for the lives of these new believers, since shipwreck seemed to be inevitable, Grimonia prayed for their physical lives to be saved. Slowly the time between thunder and lightning lessened and it became obvious that the storm was moving further away from them.

A much more cheerful crew of sailors arrived with Grimonia and Proof at Gaul. There it is said that Grimonia and Proof were under the protection of the Emperor Valentinian. However, still fearing the reach of their parents, the girls wanted solitude. They also seem to have split up at this point, but we are unclear of the details. Proof went a short distance further south compared to Grimonia, while Grimonia went into the middle of the forest of Thiérache. She stopped in a place called Dorunum in Picardy. It is now called La Capelle. La Capelle is from the Picard word for 'chapel', as a chapel was built there and dedicated to Grimonia.

In La Capelle, Grimonia was happy for a time. Grimonia had always loved the woods and forests around her home in Ireland, so was equally at home in the forest of Thiérache. In Ireland, those in her father's kingdom called her the 'bluebell girl' for her eyes were a beautiful violet-blue, the colour of bluebells ('Coinnle Corra' in Irish). And from about April every springtime, she used to delight in racing into the woods beside her home. Above her head was the newly forming leaf canopy of the trees. Then, from the vast carpets of blue, she would pick the first bluebells for her mother, the Queen. Some said the fairies wouldn't be happy at that, but Grimonia believed in Christ's protection and never let that stop her from picking them! In Gaul, when she arrived at Thiérache, she remembered how she would bend down and count the drooping tubular bells. Some had five flowers, some up to 12.

Now, in our story, an entire autumn, winter and spring had passed since Grimonia and Proof fled Ireland. Grimonia, the 'bluebell girl', was still feeling a little homesick for Ireland. Imagine her delight when summer came and the fields of Thiérache and all of Picardy became alive with blue flowers! Yes, Grimonia was delighted! Everywhere she looked, even among the wheatfields, Grimonia saw not bluebells, but cornflowers ('le bleuet' in French). She thanked God for sending her a little colour and reminder that blue, like God, was everywhere. So maybe this 'bluebell girl' would fit into life at Gaul after all?

> Today I wandered through the forest, feeling a little blue,
> I'd left home in Ireland wondering what on earth to do,
> But as the birds flew through the trees,
> The wind picked up into a breeze,

I thought of the storm that brought me to Gaul,
The white waves so high they towered like a wall,
Then at the fields beside me, I gave a glance,
And in a moment, I danced a dance,
For in line after line, blue did shine,
Then I knew in a flash, this fine land was mine.

But as is so common in tales from long ago, our story takes an unpleasant turn after this. Grimonia's father, you see, had sent men out searching for her with orders to bring her back alive – or dead! He was a cruel and heartless monstrosity of a man. It only took a short time before the men tracked Grimonia down to the ship that had left Ireland for Gaul. When they arrived in Gaul, they soon heard of a virtuous young Irish girl who lived in the forest. When they arrived at the place Grimonia was living, they tried to persuade her to come back to Ireland with them, but she would have none of it. Furious with anger, and unable to change Grimonia's mind, they launched themselves at her and cut off her head! They were cruel heartless men too. The blow was fast and clean, so Grimonia did not suffer and the men from her father then hid her body below some soil before returning to Ireland.

Proof (or Holy Proof as she was later called) met the same grim fate. The men who followed her beheaded her in the Tausson Valley, at the foot of St Vincent's Abbey, near Laon. Their bodies had met a grisly end, but their eternal souls were in heaven.

It is written that the body of Grimonia was found preserved and that miracles happened near it. Along with Proof's body, it was taken to Laquielles in 1231 by Bishop Anselm de Mauny. They are there now in the Church of St John the Baptist of Lesquielles. There is a parish and village ('commune' in French) near Laon named after Proof; it is called Sainte-Preuve (her name in French). La Capelle and Sainte-Preuve are both communes (villages) in the modern Aisne department in Hauts-de-France, in northern France.

You may well ask, why did God allow such a spine-chilling, brutal end to Grimonia and Proof's lives? It is not actually possible to understand why terrible things happen. It seems pointless that God rescued Grimonia from her father's prison only to be killed so cruelly later on. After all, it says in the Bible:

118

'For I know the plans I have for you,' declares the Lord, 'plans to prosper you and not to harm you, plans to give you hope and a future...'
– Jeremiah 29:11, NIV

But if you think about Grimonia's short life, God did have a plan for her. She got to share the amazing story of her escape from prison, helped by an angel, with all those around her, including the sailors. Their lives were then completely changed after the journey to Gaul.

Perhaps a famous quote from the time of the Roman persecution of Christians also helps. Quintus Septimius Florens Tertullianus (better known as Tertullian) wrote the following:

The blood of the martyrs is the seed of the church.

Tertullian was a prolific early Christian author and apologist from Carthage in the Roman province of Africa. He wrote during a time when Christians were regularly executed in terrible repulsive ways (e.g. fed to the lions)! The literal meaning of a 'martyr' is someone who is killed for 'bearing witness' to their faith.

See if you can think of a way that the deaths of those killed for being Christians is 'the seed of the church'.

Learn about nature

The bluebell is the sweetest flower
That waves in summer air:
Its blossoms have the mightiest power
To soothe my spirit's care.

This poetry was written by the famous writer and poet, Emily Brontë (d. 1848). Her father, Patrick Branty, was from Co. Down. Her poem says the bluebell flower made her happy! It is good for your health to spend time in nature and learn about it.

120

Perhaps you could go outside and look at the flowers or pick some? You could get a library book out on flowers. Ask yourself, what are your top five favourite flowers?

❊ **Feast days for St Grimonia** (Sainte Grimonie): 7th September (main), 20th April, Pentecost Tuesday.

❊ **Feast days for St Holy Proof** (Sainte Preuve, Santa Proba): 20th & 28th April.

❊ Some people think that St Proof lived a long time after Grimonia (fifth or sixth century). In that case, they would never have met. Others think that they both lived in the fifth or sixth century.

❊ The bluebell used to be used in bookbinding, and in setting the tail feathers on arrows ('fletching').

❊ In medieval Ireland there were the terms 'buga' and 'bó muc' for some kind of blue flower, but we don't know what that might have been!

❊ The 'bleuet de France', the blue cornflower, is used as a symbol for war victims in France.

❊ Gaul was a very popular place for Irish monks and nuns to go to as missionaries! There were over fifty Irish saint missionaries in medieval times in Gaul. At least nine of those were female.

❊ There were several Irish female cephalophores in Gaul! For example, Maxentia of Beauvais (Sainte Maxence in French). A pagan suitor followed this princess and she was beheaded! She then carried her head, still living, to a place now called Pont-Sainte-Maxence. Often, the severed heads of these cephalophore saints preached to those around them.

121

Intrepid Ia

Ia was an Irish princess. We don't know where Ia lived in Ireland, but we do know that this princess didn't want to sit in a castle all day, sewing, painting or doing whatever else princesses did! St Patrick had told her family all about God, so they wanted to share their faith of Christianity with others. They had decided to travel to Cornwall, right at the very bottom southwest coast of England. Now Cornwall is famous for its tin mining (tin is a useful silver-coloured metal that is added to copper to make bronze. It's also the main ingredient in pewter). All Irish sailors knew the way from Ireland to Cornwall, as the tin from Cornwall was traded with other countries.

One summer morning, Ia went down to the seashore to leave for Cornwall. However, she was utterly dismayed to find that her family had gone without her! Even her brothers, Uny (or Euny) and Erc (or Erth) had left her behind. They probably thought she was too young for a dangerous journey. Ia, you see, was the youngest in her family. Are you the youngest in your family or do you know someone who is the youngest in their family? Do they get treated differently because they are younger?

Disappointed and upset, Ia started to pray. She was intrepid (which means she was fearless, brave and courageous). If God wanted her to go to Cornwall, then He would have to make a way for it to happen. And Ia wasn't scared to go there (even on her own).

Then, the most amazing thing *did* happen. Her eye was drawn to a small leaf floating on the water and, without really thinking about it, she prodded it with a stick to see if it would sink. As she watched, it grew! The midvein stretched and stretched, then the little secondary veins growing out from it stretched and stretched. What a lot of straining and stretching! And as the stretching continued, the green tissue in between miraculously filled the ever-increasing diameter of the once-small leaf. It grew so large that as the sides curled up, the whole thing looked like a green boat! The leaf was now hard as a board and *huge*.

Ia could see that already this was a miracle. A strange miracle, but a miracle no less! Even though she was young, she knew that faith is about taking risks, so out she stepped onto the leaf to see what would happen. And before she knew it, she was carried right across the Irish and Celtic Seas! She travelled quickly, *really* fast, passing boats on the way. Can't you just imagine the looks on the fishermen's faces?

☞ *Imagine that you are Ia sailing to Cornwall on a leaf. Who do you think you would see on the way? Would you sit or would you be brave and stand on the leaf?*

✤ ✤ ✤

The leaf travelled *so* fast that Ia reached Cornwall before her family! It floated into a beautiful, large bay with a sandy beach. It was on the far west of this bay within a little cove that Ia first set foot on Cornish sand. The local fishermen and their families stood with their mouths open. What an impression her leaf-boat made!

As she waited for her brothers, she wandered down past sand dunes, going south to what was the mouth of the River Hayle. When the people told her she was at Hayle, she knew she was definitely in the right place as the Hayle Estuary, which is what the mouth of the river was called, was where her brothers were going. Hayle comes from the Cornish word 'Heyl', meaning 'estuary'. It was a beautiful place with lots of birds, especially wetland birds. They were all familiar to her. Everywhere around her were black and white oystercatchers ('Roilleach' in Irish) and Ia loved their distinctive long, orange-red bills and reddish-pink legs. There were lots of ducks too, including the mallard ('Lacha Fhiáin' in Irish) of course.

When her brothers finally arrived, they were utterly amazed to hear the story about her journey on the leaf. And since they now knew it was God's will for young Ia to be with them, they were very sorry that they had left her behind. But they were also completely ecstatic that she had been brought by a leaf from God! In time, they joined up with other Christian missionaries, St Gwinear (or Fingar) and St Piala (or Phiala), an Irish brother and sister who were a prince and princess. Among the group was also St Felec. Their numbers grew so large that it is said Ia and her brothers had 777 other Christians with them, and that they started new churches.

123

Sadly, there isn't much information about St Ia that survived. However, we know she worked for many years and built at least several churches. We know also that a local landlord called Dinan built a church at her request. She is also said to have built a church near the village of Troon, about 6-7 miles (10-11 km) east of the Hayle Estuary. Ia is also the patroness of the village of Plouyé, in the department of Finistère, in Brittany, Gaul (modern-day France, remember). This perhaps indicates that Ia and her companions went to France too (there is a story that Gwinear and Piala might have gone there).

Ia's brothers also started churches in the same area, all around the River Hayle Estuary. Her brother St Erc (or Erth) was not only leader of the church in Slane, Co. Meath, but had a village and church named after him by the Hayle Estuary. Her brother St Uny started churches in that part of Cornwall too, and is the patron saint of the churches in Lelant (just to the west of the Hayle Estuary) and Redruth (10 miles or 16 km northeast). Their friend, St Gwinear, has a village, civil parish and church named after him 2 miles (3 km) east of the Hayle Estuary. What a lot of churches and villages!

As well as telling the people of the area about Jesus, Ia loved going for walks and exploring the area. One day, she walked up the Red River that was flowing into the north of the bay. It had this name because Cornwall's famous tin was mined up the river, so the water flowed red from the iron oxide by-product. But her favourite place to walk was up the Hayle River in winter when it came alive with the waterfowl who overwintered on the estuary. She had always loved birds, so it was a paradise for her! There were ducks everywhere, especially Teal ('Praslacha' in Irish) and Wigeon ('Rualacha' in Irish). She loved hearing and seeing the Curlew ('Crotach' in Irish), with their distinctive shrill cry and their long, curved bills.

Often, she'd walk further still, going the short distance west to Trencrom Hill. It was in the woods below there that she first met rabbits and hedgehogs, as there were absolutely none of these creatures in Ireland! She really thought they were delightful animals! You see, it was only from the time of the Normans in the late twelfth century onwards that these animals were brought to Ireland. In Trencrom Woods, Ia listened to the birdsong and remembered the Irish names for all the birds. So many of them had names that described them perfectly. She was enjoying learning Cornish and loved that some of the words were very similar. Badger is 'broc' in Irish, but 'brogh' in Cornish, which is only slightly different. It made

SAINT BRIGID & OTHER AMAZING IRISH WOMEN

talking to the Cornish people about Jesus so much easier when their words were similar. Ia also loved her own Irish language. But she wasn't that homesick, as she had her brothers with her after all. Still, she would say the names of these birds as they flew past, to hear Irish spoken out loud again. These are modern Irish words in our story, but we can imagine that they might have been similar to what they were in Old Irish. Chaffinch ('Rí Rua' meaning 'Red king'), goldfinch ('Lasair Choille' meaning 'Bright flame of the forest'), bullfinch ('Corcrán Coille' meaning 'Little scarlet one of the woods'), jay ('Scréachóg Choille' meaning 'Screecher of the woods'). Can you see how these Irish bird names describe these birds so well? You might need to look at photos of these birds to help with some of them!

When Ia climbed up to the top of Trencrom Hill, she visited the cairns and heard the local story about its giant called Trecobben. Ia told the people about the stories of Fionn mac Cumhaill (Finn McCool). Some said he was an Irish giant, after all! From Trencrom Hill, Ia saw all around the Penwith area of west Cornwall from the north to the south coast. She could see the beautiful island called St Michael's Mount miles away to the south. On St Michael's Mount lived another Cornish giant, called Cormoran, with his wife Cormelian (until she was killed by the giant Trecobben)! Sometimes Ia would walk on further to the northwest, to Trink Hill, and on that hill there was a large granite stone called the Twelve O'Clock Rock. It was said that it could be rocked and moved, but only at midnight. Ia loved the Cornish people and how they were so similar to the people of her home in Ireland, both with cairns and stories of magical rocks and giants! It was because she loved the Cornish people so much that she did so well bringing them to a new faith in Christianity.

Sadly, Ia wasn't just a wonder woman for giving up her palace life for a missionary's life in Cornwall. She became a martyr for God (along with St Piala and some of the others). The local king had her killed one day when she was out walking by the River Hayle. It was one of her favourite places to be, so the King knew where to find her. That king was Tewdwr Mawr. He had been exiled from Brittany in Gaul (France), and now had his castle at Conerton. Conerton was near the village of Gwithian, about 3 miles (5 km) northeast of the Hayle Estuary (and just south of the Red River). Tewdwr Mawr had become increasingly antagonistic to the Irish Christians. He really hated them and was known for killing many of them. There were still lots who didn't believe in Christianity in Cornwall, you see.

But Ia remained intrepid to the end. Knowing how much she loved birds, the birds in Hayle Estuary especially, perhaps she thought of a Bible verse like this when she saw the King's men approach her:

> *He will cover you with his feathers,*
> *and under his wings you will find refuge.*
> – Psalm 91:4, NIV

Ia and her adventures were never forgotten. She was buried at the cove where her leaf-boat first floated onto Cornish sand. St Ia's Church was then built over Ia's grave, and the town of St Ives grew up around it. The town is named after her, as St Ives in Cornish is 'Porth Ia', which means 'St Ia's cove'. The cove is the small bay within the larger bay. The larger bay too is also named after Ia, as it's called St Ives Bay. Ia's holy well, Venton Ia, is near Porthmeor beach just to the north of St Ives. And Ia is still very much remembered in St Ives! *Saint Ia Rides a Leaf* is a board book for toddlers written by Melinda Johnson.

126

Alder, apple, ash, aspen, beech, birch, cherry, elm, hawthorn, hazel, holly, horse-chestnut, maple, oak, poplar, sycamore, whitebeam and willow. Some well-known, and some lesser-known trees! Try to learn the leaf shape of as many trees as you can. Not all the trees listed were around in Ireland when St Ia lived (some were introduced from other places), but don't let that spoil your fun! In St Ives, the story is that Ia crossed the sea on an ivy leaf. Go outside and collect a sample of each leaf type that you can find!

Next, paint your leaves and press them down on paper. Use crayons as well to make etchings. If it is autumn, why not paint or etch them in a mixture of autumn colours (green, red, brown, orange and yellow), then cut around the leaf shapes? Use your favourite leaf to make a drawing or collage of St Ia travelling over the Irish and Celtic Seas! Perhaps the leftover leaves can be taken into school to show your teacher.

DID YOU KNOW?

127

* Feast days: 3rd February (main) & 18th September (not celebrated anymore).
* Other names: Hya, Hia and Eia.
* Ia's sister might have been St Dahalin of Co. Kerry (Dazzling Dahalin)!
* St Piala/Phiala's feast days: Sunday closest to 21st November, 23rd February, 23rd March, 18th September & 14th December (not celebrated anymore).
* Another female Irish saint who went to Cornwall in the fifth or sixth century was St Breage (or Breaca).
* There is a long history of settlement in the Hayle Estuary area dating from the Bronze Age, but the Domesday survey in 1086 shows that the town of Hayle was not yet in existence.
* The Hayle Estuary is especially important for birds. It is in the Hayle Estuary and Carrack Gladden Site of Special Scientific Interest. The Royal Society for the Protection of Birds (RSPB) manages a nature reserve at the site.
* The fifth-century Cunaide Stone was discovered in the area of Hayle in 1843. It is thought that it might be Irish. It says on it, 'Here in peace has rested Cunat-do [or Cunaide]. Here he lies in the tomb. He lived for thirty-three years.' But some historians think Cunaide was a woman, not a man!

Inspirational Íte

Young Deirde, as she had been baptised, grew up in a royal family in Co. Waterford. That is in the southeast of Ireland, in the province of Munster. Right from when she was a girl, she showed that she was special, as she was said to have possessed the six ancient virtues of Irish womanhood! These were wisdom, purity, beauty, musical ability, gentle speech and embroidery skills.

As well as that, Íte had a very strong faith in God. She regularly fasted (went without food) and prayed. Once as a girl, when she was sleeping, everyone saw a wonderful light shining from her face. She looked like an angel! Another time, an angel actually appeared to her and gave her three precious gems. The angel taught her about the Holy Trinity through those three stones: the Father, Son (Jesus) and Holy Spirit. Indeed, Deirdre led such a holy life and desired to know God so much, that at some point she gained her other name, Íte, which means 'thirst for holiness'.

It was no surprise that when she came of age her father, Ceann Faoladh, and mother, Feidhealm (or Neacht) wanted their precious daughter to marry well. Indeed, her father was descended from a king of Tara in Co. Meath, who was the High King of the whole of Ireland. That probably put extra weight upon him to arrange for Íte to marry another noble. However, like so many of our wonder women, Íte refused to marry anyone. She fasted and prayed as was her usual custom. On this particular occasion, she fasted for three days and nights. Then, to Íte's delight, an angel appeared to her father and explained to him what a great life Íte would have serving God, and that she was to move to another part of Ireland. At this, her father allowed her to go away at once!

Íte and her sister Fiona set off. Íte was just a teenager at sixteen years old, but she was ready for an adventure! God, of course, led the way, as three lights in the sky showed them which way to travel. The first was at the top of the Galtee

Mountains. They appeared to be going in a west-northwest direction. They looked around once they got there, and sure enough, another light shone in the sky over the Mullaghareirk Mountains (in the Sliabh Luachra area). They travelled roughly west this time. When they got there, finally the light stayed over a place north of them, called Cluain Credail ('holy meadow'). Overall, they were now far to the west of Waterford and in Co. Limerick.

The local chieftain offered her a large amount of land, but Íte would only accept four acres; just enough for her monastery's needs. She got busy straight away and founded a community there. She also planted a garden and grew vegetables. If you had a garden that you could plant vegetables in, what would YOU grow?

In time, Íte's community became known as Killeedy (Cell Íte, 'Church of Ita'). She also started another community nearby, to the northeast at Kilmeedy ('Church of my Ita'). What a lot of directions! If you drive from Waterford City to Killeedy today by car it is about 100 miles (161 km). Some people think that she left from the barony of Decies-without-Drum in Co. Waterford. If that were true, it would have been a slightly shorter journey, but not by much. What a long journey Íte and her sister Fiona had!

As well as teaching those who joined her community (which was probably for both women and men), Íte had a school for little boys at Killeedy. She became the foster-mother of many saints. Fostering was common then in that time of Ireland's history. Let's look at a register of some of her pupils to see how they turned out!

❀ **St Mo Chóemóc.** He was one of her nephews. She also resurrected his father from the dead after a battle by reattaching his head! She was a funny foster-mum, as she gave him the nickname Pulcherius, as he was handsome. 'Pulcher' is Latin for 'beautiful'. He founded a monastery in Liathmore, Co. Tipperary.

❀ **St Cumm...éne Fota.** He became a brilliant theologian who studied God. No doubt this was because of his early days spent with Íte. He had over forty manuscripts in his library of holy books, which was a huge number back then!

❀ **St Brendan the Navigator.** He stayed with Íte for five years, from when he was one until he was six. Not only did he start monasteries like Clonfert in Co. Galway, he went on a famous seven-year voyage around the Atlantic Ocean discovering all sorts of unusual islands too! Even though he'd been young, Brendan never forgot Íte and visited her between voyages.

Once, he asked her what three things God loved best. Íte said, 'True faith in God and a pure heart, a simple life with a religious spirit and open-handedness inspired by charity.' Another time Brendan asked her what three things God most detested. She said: 'a scowling face, obstinacy in wrongdoing, and too great a confidence in the power of money.'

☞ *Can you explain in your own words what Íte meant, and do you agree with her?*

❖ ❖ ❖

Well, they all turned out very well, so Íte must have done an excellent job!

Íte also became known for many wonderful miracles. Here are just some of them! Once a local chieftain sent an urgent message: there was a 5,000 strong army from neighbouring Co. Kerry and they were only a relatively short distance away to the west, at Abbeyfeale. They looked like they wanted a battle! Íte told the Limerick soldiers to repent of their sins, and so they did. Íte prayed as the two armies clashed. All day they fought. The Limerick soldiers were fewer in number and should have been slaughtered, but Íte had been praying for them the whole time, and so the defeated Kerry men fled for their homes by sunset!

Íte had a lovely little donkey ('Asal' in Irish) who worked very hard. Every day Íte and her donkey went on a long journey to the pastures of Seeconglass, near Mountcollins to the southwest. It was about 10 miles (16 km) away. That just shows you how hardworking Íte and her little donkey were! After the cows were milked, Íte made the return journey with her donkey and the milk. What a long trip it was indeed! One day, as she was on the way home from getting the milk, she heard that there was a sick man in Tournafulla (which was on her way home), so she stopped to help him. Someone else might not have bothered, as it was such a long and tiring journey, but Íte, being so caring, decided to visit him. Now, while she was inside the sick man's house, her poor donkey was awfully treated by the villagers. He was beaten and some boys threw stones at him. He went running off into the River Allaghaun, spilling the milk everywhere! It is said that when her donkey stood on a big rock by the river, the donkey's feet sank into the surface and that to this day his hoof marks (and Íte's footprints) can still be seen. In another version of the story, it was a cruel man who set his dogs on Íte's donkey. When Íte came out of the sick man's house and found out what had happened, she was furious and cursed the

131

people of Tournafulla! But, people say that if anyone who is sick stands in the rock by the river, they will be healed.

In another story, Íte pulled out a thorn from her donkey's hoof. Then she planted it and it grew into a tree.

There are also many other stories about her fasting (going without food), successfully praying for people to be healed, supernaturally identifying a thief, and knowing what people were thinking! On one occasion, she was miraculously transported to Clonmacnoise, Co. Offaly, to receive Holy Communion (or the Eucharist or Mass). She didn't travel by boat up the River Shannon! No, God transported her about 100 miles (161 km) up Ireland – the same distance as Íte and her sister Fiona walked from Waterford to Co. Limerick. But this time, there was no walking. It was a completely supernatural journey. She then returned home to Killeedy the same miraculous way that very same day!

Íte was such a kind and caring person that there is the following incredibly strange story. As the story goes, she once let a stag beetle as 'big as a lap-dog' eat 'the whole of one of her sides'! Another scholar mentioned the idea that it was a sort of leech-like worm, called a Daol! Whatever it was, Íte put up with this and didn't let anyone know! But one day, the nuns at Killeedy saw the beetle and of course they killed it straight away. However, most historians say this story was symbolic. Perhaps the writer of the story used it to explain that she had a cancerous tumour near the end of her life. Indeed, there are two dates given for Íte's death (570 and 579). This might show that in general not much was known about the circumstances and details of her death.

The story continues that Íte then missed the stag beetle and became very sad. It is said that Íte asked God to send her the Christ child (Jesus) to foster and he was sent to her as an infant! It was then that she is said to have written a lullaby poem for the infant Jesus, called 'Ísucán' (Little Jesus). It begins, 'Little Jesus who is in fosterage with me in my little hermitage.'

The Martyrology of Óengus described Íte as, 'the white sun of Munster's women'. Íte was so famous throughout the world that she is also known as 'Brigid of Munster'. An extra reason why this shouldn't surprise is that she was said to be St Brigid of Kildare's cousin. According to the Tract on the Mothers of the Saints, Íte's mum, Feidhealm (or Neacht), was a sister of Brigid's mum, Broicseach.

In the ninth century, Vikings raided Íte's monastery and it was destroyed. However, people today still visit her grave and holy wells. There are four in southwest Limerick.

'An eye for an eye'

Íte's famous ancestor was High King of Ireland, Felim the lawgiver (Fedlimid Rechtmar), who is said to have instituted the principle of 'an eye for an eye' into Irish law. After that, the behaviour of the Irish people is said to have improved! This rule is also in the Old Testament part of the Bible (Exodus 21:23–27), but Jesus urged his followers to 'turn the other cheek':

You have heard that it was said, 'Eye for eye, and tooth for tooth.' But I tell you, do not resist an evil person. If anyone slaps you on the right cheek, turn to them the other cheek also.
(Matthew 5:38-39, NIV)

What do you think Jesus meant?

DID YOU KNOW?

133

❋ Feast day: 15th January.

❋ Other names: Íde, Ita, Mida, Ida, Ides and Deirdre.

❋ There is a stained-glass window designed by Michael Healy in the National Gallery of Ireland. It shows Íte with St Brendan as a boy holding a toy boat! I wonder if Íte had been telling him bedtime stories of sailing adventures?

❋ Íte's sister, Fiona, had a son called Flan of Ossa. He became King of Northumbria in present day England.

❋ Íte was taught as a child about God as the Trinity. One modern way to understand the Trinity is to think of water. Water has three states: solid ice, liquid water and gas (which is also called steam). They are distinctive but all are water.

❋ Despite the donkey being an iconic image of Irish rural life, it appears to have been little used in Ireland before the eighteenth century. There is no native word for donkey; the Irish 'Asal' comes instead from Latin asselus 'little ass'!

Lovely Lí Ban

LOUGH NEAGH ❧ 3ᴿᴰ - 6ᵀᴴ CENTURY

It was a lovely spring morning with a slight mist in the air, which was always a sign of a beautiful day to come. Everything was calm in Princess Lí Ban's home at the royal castle in the middle of Ulster. Ulster is the province in the north of Ireland. Her father was King Eochaid (also spelt Eochu), king of half of Ulster, and son of King Mairid of Munster (in the south of Ireland). Her mother was called Queen Eibhliu and had two brothers, called Conaing and Curnan. Lí Ban, like every princess in this book, was both beautiful and enchanting. In fact, she was so lovely that her name meant 'beauty of women'.

Bright and early, Lí Ban had risen from her bed and run down to the caves below the castle. Armed with a blanket, candles and her fishing net, Lí Ban was all set for a fun day catching fish in the waters near her home. Her little Irish terrier pup followed eagerly behind her. 'Madra' ('dog' in Irish), as she called him, had not been born long so hadn't even been given his own name, but Lí Ban liked the name 'Madra', and thought it might just suit him. And besides, she was waiting for inspiration to name him something else, and none had struck yet! And like all good dogs, wherever Lí Ban went, Madra always went too.

Lí Ban had a special cave that was all hers, or at least that was Lí Ban's opinion. In her mind, it was her secret place. Down she ran, squeezing into the entrance and then back up a shaft into her own special hideaway. She laid her blanket down on her makeshift bed at the back wall, then rolled up her sleeves ready for a day's enjoyment of catching the biggest fish she could find. Lí Ban's cave, you see, was fed by waters from the upper River Bann, so it had lots of fish in it. Down from the headwaters it came to Lí Ban's home, from Slieve Muck Mountain in the Mournes of Co. Down.

Lí Ban planned to take the fish back home for her father's palace Cook to prepare for their evening meal. Yet, in a flash the hours rolled in until, without

SAINT BRIGID & OTHER AMAZING IRISH WOMEN

realising the time, Lí Ban yawned and putting her day's catch by her bed, she lay down just for a few minutes (that was her plan anyway). Little did Lí Ban know, life changing events would occur as she slept!

Lí Ban awoke to a crashing noise at the ceiling of the cave. That was the first sign that something significant had occurred. A shaft of sunlight now streamed down into her secret room, where before the cave had been completely enclosed. There was also an extremely loud gushing noise all around, as if water were erupting everywhere. Yet Lí Ban could only guess that that was what was happening, as she could see none of it. The downwards exit from Lí Ban's cave was now flooded so she had no way out!

After some thought of the stories she knew about two giant magical peeing horses from the Irish gods, and the capped well at her home, she was soon able to work out what might have happened. Her brother was cruelly nicknamed the 'halfwit', as he had predicted that the well at her home would flood the entire area and bring catastrophe. But that is getting ahead of the story. Let me go back and retell the dreaded tale of the magical peeing horses that Lí Ban had grown up hearing. Yes, giant magical peeing horses (not many people know about this part of the story, but it is all part of Irish folklore)!

Lí Ban's family tree was a little complicated, so pay attention. Before Lí Ban was born, her mother, Eibhliu, had been married to her grandfather, the King of Munster. Yet, she was his second wife and very young; too young for him actually. Despite being the stepmother of Lí Ban's father, she and Lí Ban's father, Eochaid (her grandfather's son), fell in love! Of course, they had to flee from Munster (due to her grandfather's rage)! So off set her father, mother, and her uncle Ribh, all on horseback with some people from the kingdom who were loyal to them. As they travelled north, her uncle Ribh decided to separate, as there had been a prophecy that disaster would fall if they stayed together. Yet, calamity fell upon him anyway! The Irish god Midir was a son of the Dagda of the Tuatha Dé Danann (the Irish gods and goddesses). He was described as 'king of the north country, lord of horse breeding peoples'. Midir wanted to meddle in human affairs and so killed all the horses belonging to Ribh and his followers! However, he then replaced the horses with one of his own. Ribh and his followers climbed onto this horse from Midir, but when it stopped and did a pee, a spring erupted that drowned Ribh and his followers underwater! This body of water is now known as

Lough Ree. It is on the River Shannon in the midlands of Ireland. That's the sort of thing that happens I guess when you borrow a horse from the gods!

Then Midir's foster-son, the god Óengus, appeared and gave Eochaid and Eibhliu an absolutely ENORMOUS horse that carried all their belongings. But Óengus warned them they must not let the horse rest or it too would be their doom. However, after reaching Ulster, the horse stopped and it too did a pee. Being a magical horse from a god, of course, a spring arose from that very spot! Ignoring the warning from the god Óengus, Eochaid decided to build a house there. He covered the spring with a capstone to stop it overflowing and placed an old woman in charge of it. He thought that left the problem solved. The years passed without any problems, and everyone was lulled into a false sense of security. Little did they know that, years later, the night when young Lí Ban had fallen asleep safely down in an underground cave, that the capstone of the magical well was *not* replaced. You see, the old woman had forgotten to do her job! And so the spring overflowed. Young Lí Ban at this point did not know her father, mother and most of the household had been *drowned*! Neither did she know that beside her cave hideaway there was now the biggest lough in the whole of Ireland – and Britain! This lough was Lough Neagh (Loch nEathach in Irish, 'Eochu's lake', named after Lí Ban's father).

Well, as you can imagine, it took many days for Lí Ban, trapped in her cave, to come to terms with her solitude and the knowledge that the prophecy from her brother Curnan seemed to have come true. Thankfully, she had everything she needed in her hideaway. In fact, it seemed the gods and goddesses had looked favourably upon her, as the new opening in the roof that had formed let sunlight in and provided fresh air to breath. She fished by day and had some candles to light at night. Madra her little lap dog did a super job of keeping her company. But months passed; soon, a year went past. Lí Ban was now in despair of ever getting out. She saw the salmon and trout, little sticklebacks and long slinky eels, and wished and wished that she could be free to wonder in and out of the cave like them. When she reached her lowest point and utterly despaired though, she had the most amazing encounter with none other than the god Manannán mac Lir, the god of the sea! He suddenly rose up from the cave's pool of water one day and announced to Lí Ban that she had been and would continue to be under his protection. He knew of Lí Ban's wish to be free like the salmon ('Bradán' in Irish) and said he could grant her wish. But it would mean that she would be half-salmon! Lí Ban sighed, 'Oh, to be like the merrow you mean! A mermaid! I don't want to be like a selkie with a cap that can be taken by people so that I can't get back to sea. I would like to be a mermaid, with a beautiful silvery salmon tail and able to breath both air and under water!'

'Very well, your wish is granted,' Manannán mac Lir said. 'The salmon is king of the fish and the wisest of all Irish animals, so that is a fitting choice! You will be like the gods and goddesses and live for hundreds of years if you so desire' Manannán mac Lir said all this with a swoosh of light and water, and a wave of his powerful sword, Fragarach ('The Whisperer', 'The Answerer' or 'The Retaliator') in the air. And so the god of the sea transformed Lí Ban into the mermaid, which she would be for many hundreds of years. But then Lí Ban, transformed into half-salmon, remembered her little pup, Madra, and asked what could be done for him. He was such a good, loyal little dog after all and went everywhere with Lí Ban. So Manannán transformed him into a 'Madra Uisce', literally a 'water dog' in Irish, or otter, since his name was Madra and he needed to be able to swim underwater!

Lí Ban and Madra dived down into the water of the cave and joined Manannán in his chariot, led by Enbarr, his magical horse. Down, down the chariot dived through the deep water, until they surfaced in what was a giant lough. It bordered a huge area of Ulster; what is now Co. Down, Armagh, Tyrone, Derry and Antrim. It wasn't just one of the twelve chief loughs in Ireland as it was called long ago in the past, but THE chief lough! Across Lough Neagh they went in the chariot. Nothing of Li Ban's former home could be seen. Instead, there were a few dotted islands of raised land in the lough and just a massive expanse of still freshwater. The sea god went north to the edge of the lough to what is now Toome in Co. Antrim, and further northwards they travelled up the lower River Bann, right out to the Atlantic Ocean to what is now Barmouth, between Portstewart and Castlerock in Co. Derry. Manannán waved Lí Ban and Madra goodbye and said he would come back to see her over the years whenever she wished. His departing words were, 'Enjoy my breaking waves against the shore!' Lí Ban wondered slightly at what he meant. In early Irish, the breaking waves were known as 'graig mic lir' ('the horses of (Manannán) mac Lir'). She knew that much, but hadn't been to the seashore very often in her young life and so didn't comprehend the full significance of his words, even as she looked out at the breaking water at Portstewart.

Lí Ban and Madra swam eastwards a short distance until they reached the breathtaking sight of the Giant's Causeway on the north coast of Co. Antrim. She had heard of this place with its many-sided stones in their thousands; about 40,000 to be precise! Most of the stone columns were hexagonal (six-sided), although there are also some with four, five, seven or eight sides. They reached down from the high cliff to the sea. Lí Ban and Madra peered up in awe at the stones; they really must be one of the natural wonders of the world, Lí Ban thought. Or perhaps Fionn mac Cumhaill (Finn McCool) had made them, as was said in fireside stories. On and on around Ireland's coast they swam. Not just the causeway coastal route, but down the east and up the west. It was then at Ireland's southern tip, where the sea met the Atlantic Ocean crashing onto the shore, that it dawned on Lí Ban what the sea god had meant about his waves being his horses. And that day Lí Ban understood what he had meant (and possibly predicted) was the day Lí Ban became not just a mermaid, but a surfing mermaid!

It was at Kinsale, Co. Cork, where Lí Ban (and Madra her otter) were first spotted by a human, surfing the waves coming into shore. Even today there are stories of her, especially where she was seen surfing! She worked her way up the west coast along what is now called the Wild Atlantic Way. Co. Kerry, then Aileens, Lahinch, Co. Clare. Wow! The Aileens, as they are called, are found at the foot of the Cliffs of Moher. These famous sea cliffs run for about 14 km (9 miles) and reach a towering height of 214 m (702 ft). Lí Ban loved swimming out past the reef and surfing back in under the huge tunnels of waves. In and out she'd swim over and over every day! Then, up past Co. Galway to Co. Sligo. At Easky, there were two amazing reef breaks, one to the left next to the river mouth (where a river flows into a bigger pool of water, like a lake or the sea) and one going right, near where there is a castle now. Then, up to Mullaghmore Head, Co. Sligo. In recent times, waves up to 15 metres (49 ft) high have been recorded here. In October 2020, Mullaghmore came even closer to the record, as a wave measuring 18.2 metres (60 ft) was recorded off its coast. Further north, she went up to Co. Donegal, to what is now called 'The Peak' at Bundoran. The tallest wave ever recorded in Ireland was here in December 2011. It was 20.4 metres (67 ft) high! Lí Ban knew about all these tallest waves from hundreds of years of surfing. These were all some of Lí Ban's favourite surfing spots, as they are for today's surfers! But surfing wasn't the only thing she did.

Once a year it was as if her half-salmon instinct took over, as Lí Ban became homesick for Lough Neagh. She had remembered where the sandbar near Portstewart was, at the mouth of the River Bann, and so up the 38 miles (61 km) of the lower Bann she swam with the salmon every year. There were not many people in Ireland long ago when Lí Ban lived, and there was much more forest, but Lí Ban still made this journey at dusk, night or very early morning. In through the brackish, salty, sandbar mouth, then past the Cutts south of Coleraine, Carnroe weir, the Betts, Culiff Rock, Movanagher weir, Portna, Kilrea, and then the entrance into Lough Neagh at Toome! Like the kingly salmon, Lí Ban could leap higher than a man, even up over the weirs, where Lí Ban knew to be extra wary of humans. The fishermen on the river knew to fish with their wickerwork baskets just below the weirs. This was where the salmon gathered to rest in the richly oxygenated water before leaping up over the weirs. Like the salmon on their mission, Lí Ban also travelled on an empty stomach.

Lí Ban ventured up each of the rivers flowing into Lough Neagh. She had plenty of time and was curious to know where the salmon went. She swam up the Clady, Agivey, Moyola, Ballinderry, Maine and the Six Mile Water. Her salmon friends went back to their river homes to breed, and sadly to die. Over half the year, there were salmon coming back home in early May, with stragglers even past mid-December making the journey too.

Then, of course, Lí Ban was curious about the many eels ('Eascann' in Irish) in the lough. Where did the eels go to? So off she swam on an even greater voyage! She travelled all the way southwest of Ireland, down to the Sargasso Sea in the far southwest of the North Atlantic Ocean. She discovered that the eels were born there and then, once matured, migrated back to the Sargasso Sea to spawn and lay their own eggs, to make even more eels. Such a long voyage! She was fascinated by the eels' journey and by the vast number of sea creatures in the ocean; 'pods' of whales, 'shivers' of sharks, 'schools' of fish, and 'smucks' of jellyfish to name a few. When she saw the jellyfish ('Smugairle Róin' in Irish), she laughed and giggled at its meaning in Irish, which is 'Seal Snot'. What an appropriate name!

But Lí Ban was an Irish girl at heart and preferred to stay closer to her home. Not only did she frequently return to her cave by Lough Neagh near her old castle home, but over the centuries she also craved human contact.

There are stories of her at such places as the Mermaid's Cave (Dunluce Castle, Co. Antrim), Coney Island (Co. Sligo) and Nendrum monastery (Mahee Island, Strangford Lough, Co. Down). There are also many images of mermaids, for example at Clonfert Cathedral and Clontuskert Abbey, both in Co. Galway, so humans did see her!

It was at Nendrum monastery that she first encountered the Christian monks and their message, centuries after the sea god had changed her into a mermaid. Nendrum had been founded by St Mo Choí/Cóelán (d. 497), who had been appointed by St Patrick. However, unlike the stories handed down over hundreds of years, Lí Ban did not really try to beguile Nendrum's monks. She was only curious and wanted to hear about this new religion that had recently appeared in Ireland. Nendrum's monks eagerly shared the story of Christianity to Lí Ban and over the years she wanted to hear more.

Lí Ban had now lived 300 years as a mermaid when one day she was singing, as she often did. But monks in a passing currach heard her angelic sounds and dipped down their fishing net to try and catch her. Low and behold, Lí Ban was caught for the very first time! She was caught at the mouth of the Inver River, by Larne in Co. Antrim in the year 558 AD. It was a monk called Béoán, son of Innli, who had caught her. He was with some other monks from the great St Comgall of Bangor's monastery in Co. Down on their way to deliver a message from St Comgall to Rome (in modern day Italy). Lí Ban had already heard some of the message of Christianity from the monks at Nendrum, but she was eager to hear more, so Béoán told her about the real creator God of the sea (and everything else). One of the Bible passages that Béoán mentioned especially made an impression on Lí Ban:

Praise the Lord from the earth, you great sea creatures and all ocean depths.
– Psalm 148:7, NIV

A little to Béoán's surprise, Lí Ban promised to meet him at Larne Lough (Inbhear nOllarbha) that same day in a year's time. Béoán continued on his voyage to Rome to consult with the Pope on matters of monastic rule. And Lí Ban had one more year to swim the seas and surf the ocean. Then, according to what she had agreed, Lí Ban kept her appointment with Béoán in Larne Lough. Currachs gathered and Lí Ban was caught in a net again. She was caught by a monk called Fergus of Downpatrick (d. 584/590) this time. To make her more comfortable, the boat was half-filled with water. In one version of the story, Lí Ban blessed a chief who was wearing a purple cloak and had offered it to her. It was the same purple colour as her father Eochaid's cloak. But there is another story that there was an ignorant oaf of a man who killed Madra, her little dog (thinking he was 'only' an otter)!

Then, a three-way dispute arose as to whom Lí Ban belonged. Fergus had caught Lí Ban in his net, she was caught in the diocese of St Comgall of Bangor, but it was with Béoán that she had first made contact. The monk Béoán was from a different monastery all together; the monastery of Tech Dabeoc (House of St Da Beóc/Dabheog, Lough Derg, Co. Donegal).

So, the monks prayed, and that night an angel told them that two stags would appear. The stags were to be hitched to a chariot and they were to put Lí Ban in the chariot. Wherever the stags stopped was where Lí Ban belonged. (In another version of the story, it is two oxen who appear, and the story occurs after Lí Ban dies). The stags brought the cart to the church of Béoán. When Lí Ban was given the choice of dying and going to heaven right away or living for another 300 years and then ascending to heaven, she chose to die immediately. For, as the famous Belfast-born writer of *The Chronicles of Narnia* wrote to a Mary Willis Shelburne in June 1963:

> *There are better things ahead than any we leave behind.*
> – C.S. Lewis (d. 1963) in *Collected Letters, Vol. III: Narnia, Cambridge, and Joy 1950–1963*, (2007).

Then St Comgall (d. 597/602) baptised Lí Ban, giving her the name Muirgein ('sea-born') or Muirgeilt ('sea-wander'). From that day, the legend says Lí Ban wrought wonders and miracles at the place she was buried – that is, Lough Derg in Co. Donegal.

❖ ❖ ❖

Lí Ban is still very much remembered, especially in Bangor, Co. Down, and there is a large mural of her by the sea front, painted by the artist Friz. In Bangor Abbey, there is a handmade quilt hanging on the transept wall and in one of its squares, you will find Lí Ban floating on the crest of a wave! Local children's book author, Marianne McShane, wrote *Rónán and the Mermaid: A Tale of Old Ireland*, which is about Lí Ban. Also, on the wall of Bangor marina there is a mosaic of St Comgall and other monks in a currach, just like the one they would have met Lí Ban in!

Under the sea...

TASK

Draw a picture of a mermaid, then write a story about her. If you can, decorate her with seashells, sequins for her tail, and wool for her long hair! Make the blue sea from blue wool or paper cut up!

DID YOU KNOW?

❋ **Feast days:** 27ᵗʰ January (main) & 18ᵗʰ December (not celebrated anymore).

❋ **Other names:** Liban, Líobhan and Fuinche.

❋ The Annals of Inisfallen date the eruption of Lough Neagh to before 68 AD. So, was Lí Ban around 500 years old? It's a mystery!

❋ Lí Ban's two brothers, Conaing and Curnan, were also saved from the flooding well. From Curnan, the 'halfwit', are descended the Dál mBuain and the Dál Sailne (important Ulster tribes from long ago).

❋ In Irish mythology, the salmon is the wisest creature as the Salmon of Knowledge ate from nine magical hazelnuts fallen into Connla's Well, the Well of Knowledge/Wisdom, somewhere near the River Boyne.

❋ In the Annals of Ulster, an entry for 890 AD records a gigantic mermaid 59.44 metres (195 ft), long and whiter than a swan. The length of her hair was 5.5 metres (18 ft)!

❋ Irish words for a mermaid: muruach, murúch, moruadh and muireoig.

❋ The Eurasian otter (or river otter), which is what Madra was, can close its ears and nose when underwater.

❋ Slemish ('Sliabh Mis', meaning 'Mis's Mountain' in Irish) in Co. Antrim, and the Slieve Mish Mountains in Co. Kerry are named after Lí Ban's aunt, Mis (her father's sister).

Lupait of the Linens

You have probably heard of St Patrick, but did you know that traditionally he is said to have had five sisters? They were Dar Erca, Lupait, Tigris, Richell and Liamain. He doesn't write about them in his own writings, but they are mentioned later on in the *Tripartite Life of St Patrick*.

Let me tell you the story of one of them: Lupait. Her father was called Calpurnius, and her mother was called Conchessa. Her mother was said to be a close relation to St Martin of Tours in Gaul, a great and holy man; she was said to be either his niece or sister. Lupait was said to have been born in a place called Nemthor (somewhere in Britain). This was probably near their home at Bannaven Taburniae. There is a story about Lupait and Patrick when they were young. One day they were out in the fields, separating the lambs from their mothers, the ewes, as it was weaning time. Lupait was running, but suddenly her foot slipped. Down she came with a crash, landing full-front on her face where there was as large stone! She had no time to put out her hand to save herself. It was an extremely serious injury and looked as if her head was fractured. Patrick was young and very upset, and was soon in tears. But he prayed and made the sign of the cross in the blood from her wound, and it healed immediately! Strangely, over time, a white mark remained where the wound had been and she always carried it on her forehead.

You might know that one day Patrick was taken captive from Britain to Ireland by pirates. However, the *Tripartite Life of St Patrick* states that Lupait and their sister, Tigris, were both taken captive too. To make matters worse, they were separated. Patrick was believed to have been held captive for six years at Slemish Mountain (Sliabh Mis), Co. Antrim, where he looked after sheep. Lupait we are told was held as a slave in the kingdom of Conaille Muirtheimne, in the area between the

145

Cooley Mountains of Co. Louth going south to the River Boyne – quite a distance south of Patrick!

The years passed, and there is a story that one day Patrick's slave owner, Milchú, brought Lupait to Patrick as a potential wife. The two had been raised all those years separately and didn't know who each was. However, as soon as Patrick saw the white mark on Lupait's forehead, he knew immediately that she was his sister! So they didn't get married!

Now, in later years when Patrick returned to Ireland after a long spell away, there were some unusual and even strange stories about Lupait. In one tale, it is said that she was immoral and had become pregnant. Patrick was tempted to drive over her three times with his chariot! It seems clear that this was a different girl called Lupait and it doesn't seem historical. Patrick would have been very unlikely to use such uncaring teaching methods!

In another, more reliable story, one of Lupait's nephews, Mel, had become an itinerant (travelling) bishop and was living on her farm. Mel was the son of Lupait's sister, Dar Erca. However, even though Mel and Lupait were nephew and aunt, there were nosy gossips around. Scandalous rumours had started that their relationship was sinful. Some people are just nasty busybodies. St Patrick went to investigate and it wasn't long before Mel and Lupait knew what to do. They both produced miracles to show Patrick and all the neighbours that they were innocent. Mel ploughed up a live fish in the middle of the field, and Lupait carried hot coal without being burned!

However, after all that, Patrick advised Lupait and Mel to live apart. With her farming skills in tow, Lupait set out towards Armagh and looked after a convent of holy women east of the city, at a place called Temple na fearta. Armagh is in the province of Ulster, in the north of Ireland. It wasn't long before the potato fields were ready for preparing for flax. Soon, Lupait would be known as Lupait of the linens!

It was April and everything was ready. The field was ploughed, cut with the disc, braked, rolled and ready for the small, silky flax seeds. Lupait wasn't just an amazing wonder woman – she wasn't afraid to get the dirt of soil on her hands and under her fingernails. Her attitude in life was that whatever she did, she was doing it for God. She agreed with this Bible verse:

Whatever you do, work at it with all your heart, as working for the Lord,
not for human masters, since you know that you will receive an inheritance
from the Lord as a reward. It is the Lord Christ you are serving.
– Colossians 3:23-24, NIV

Lupait personally put the seed into the fiddle (the machine used for sowing the flax seeds). Then up and down the field she walked. That was called broadcast sowing and is where our modern term 'broadcast of television' is from! Then it was rolled, and the magic began. In five days, the flax would be peaking through the soil. In no time, the wee blue flower appeared. It was June now. But not time to pull it just yet. Twelve weeks passed between sowing and pulling. Finally, the day came when Lupait decided the field was ready and she called some local men to help, as it was indeed hard work. The flax had to be pulled out, not cut, as some of the valuable crop was growing just below the surface of the ground. Rushes were cut with a scythe to make bands to wrap around the flax bundles (these bundles were called 'beats' and twelve beats make a 'stook'). Lupait paid the working men by the stook, the way it had always been done, and indeed would be done for many hundreds of years into the future. Ireland would be known into the twentieth century as a famous producer of flax and linen!

Then there was rippling (the removing of seed heads), and then the smelliest job of them all, the retting. The local men diverted the little stream beside the convent into a dam. Each of the stooks was forked into the water, crop-head down. The men and local boys got down into the dam and lifted out the great big stones that were used each year for this next part and the stones were set on top of the stooks, to weigh them down in the water. Lupait laughed each year when she let the local children play a wonderful game of jumping on the stepping-stones of the dam while trying not to get their feet wet, or worse, fall into the water!

Retting normally took ten to twelve days in the warmth of the summer sun, but if it had been a bad summer it took longer and things were delayed to autumn. The dam was trodden down in the morning and evening every day for those twelve days. Then the flax, with the woody part weakened, was spread out to dry in the sun. The men who lifted out the wet retted flax were stinking. They smelt like modern silage sap! Then came more fascinating terms; breaking, scutching and hacking when the outer layers were taken off. It was now time for spinning, weaving, bleaching and beetling.

It is known that Lupait was very involved in the spinning and weaving, as each evening she worked long into the night on her spinning wheel. Indeed, it became such a common job for women in Ireland that women not yet married became known as spinsters; the word comes from 'spinning'. The linen, as the flax was called now, was reeled into lengths of 300 yards, boiled in a pot over the fire, then dried. At this point Lupait could start the weaving. She had a large loom in the convent. Again, into the evenings, she sat at the loom in her bare feet. Two threads were needed and the weft yarn was put on a shuttle in her hand. Then she passed the shuttle from right to left; the weft yarn going through the warp yarn on the loom.

Next, they had to turn the cloth a spotless white, before beetling it. Beetling was the pounding and hammering that tightened the weave and gave the cloth a smoother feel. However, we know Lupait wasn't involved so much with those jobs. They were difficult activities, so some of the local men would have helped.

Finally came one of Lupait's favourite final steps in the linen process. Lupait was excellent at embroidery, or 'tambouring' as it was known. Her ability to 'flower' and 'sprig' the lovely patterns onto the linen was known far and wide. Lupait took great delight in providing her brother Patrick with linen altar cloths and vestments for his church, so it is for her weaving and embroidery that she is best known. However, knowing that Lupait was a farmer from childhood, I like to think she was involved in many more steps of the long and hard process of turning flax into linen!

One more thing we know about Lupait is that she might have been a mother. In the book on *The Mothers of the Irish Saints*, attributed to Óengus the Culdee, it is stated that she was the mother of seven sons! They were called Seachnall, Nechtán, Dabonna, Mogornan, Darigoc, Usaulle, and Lughna. Each led a church. However, it seems that things aren't clear cut, and some of those sons might actually be her nephews (their mums being Dar Erca or Liamain).

Embroid it Yourself

Try some embroidery! See if you can find a piece of
fabric, some thread and a needle. What picture could you
embroider?

DID YOU KNOW?

❊ **Feast day:** 27th September.

❊ **Other names:** Lubaid and Lupita.

❊ Making linen clothes is given as an example of one of the most important
things about being a good wife in the Old Testament of the Bible (Proverbs
31:24b).

❊ Lupait's sister, Dar Erca, had nineteen children (seventeen bishops & two
nuns)! She is the patroness of Valentia Island, Co. Kerry. Her feast day is 22nd
March.

❊ There is next to nothing known about Lupait's other sisters.

❊ In the seventeenth century, it was thought that Lupait's grave was discovered.
Her body had been buried standing up between two crosses (one in front, one
behind). Strange!

Moninne of the Mountains

Have you ever climbed a mountain? Not a hill, but a mighty mountain? Think about what it was like that day. Was it windy? Did you need to sit down and take a break on the way up? What could you see from the top? Was the view good? Were you tired afterwards? Would you climb a mountain again? Well, if you were going to start a church, would you choose a mountain for its location? Perhaps you think that's a strange, rather windy place to choose, though the view might be good! Well, this is the story of Moninne who kept on repeatedly choosing mountains for the locations of her churches. And you'll see that there were special reasons for her location in Co. Armagh in particular.

Darerca, or Sáirbhile as she was called as a girl, was from Co. Down in southeast Ulster. Her father was called Mochta and he was a King of the Uí Eachach Cobha in Co. Down. Her mum was called Cuman (the saint who had 20 or 47 children). Her mum was also the daughter of a king. So, young Darerca was a princess like so many of our amazing wonder women. Since her mum was Cuman, she had many famous members who were church leaders! One of her sisters was Darbiled of Fallmore in Co. Mayo! Two of her famous cousins were Brigid of Kildare and Íte of Killeedy in Co. Limerick. And one of her more famous aunts was Faber of Boho in Co. Fermanagh.

Now, you might ask, why was she called Darerca to begin with? Well, it is said that she was named Darerca after one of St Patrick's sisters. Then there is a story that she got her later name Moninne, since she prayed for a poet called Nimín who couldn't speak, and he was healed! His first words were, 'Ninna Ninna', which became 'Moninne'. It was also said that as a baby, Darerca's first word was 'Ninna'. The name Moninne means 'my daughter' in Irish (m'iníon).

As the great St Patrick was passing through her father's kingdom, he stopped at Moninne's parents' home and baptised Moninne at a pool named Briu (or Briughas).

We don't know where this pool was, but it was somewhere near her home. St Patrick predicted that Moninne's name would be remembered throughout time. It is also said that she was veiled by St Patrick too when she became a nun!

Now that she was a nun, Moninne was busy founding churches. She was young (only a teenager!) but she was a 'foundress'. In modern terms, you might call her a church planter. It would be her life's work, in which she was so influential that she's one of the four female Irish saints who have a Vita (Latin Life) written about them!

Moninne founded a convent of nuns in Faughart, Co. Louth (where Brigid of Kildare was born). But one night, the nuns were disturbed by sounds of very rude songs from people down the hill. It was a noisy wedding party! Also, she had found that family members kept calling on her, disturbing her focus on church work. So Moninne decided to look for a more suitable location for their convent. For a while, they spent time with St Ibar, who is said to have been Moninne's uncle. At first, they were with St Ibar on the Aran Islands in Galway Bay, in the far west of Ireland, but then they travelled with him when he moved to Beggerin Island in the Wexford slobs (which now contains a wildfowl reserve), in the far south of Ireland. Moninne also spent time with St Brigid of Kildare. Some say she was even part-raised as a girl by Brigid. So, she received the very best of training!

After much prayer about where God wanted her to lead her flock, Moninne took the spiritual battle for souls to a key site in Ireland. She moved to the beautiful setting of Slieve Gullion, 'mountain of the (steep) slope' or 'Culann's mountain'. It was the tallest mountain in Co. Armagh. And Co. Armagh, like Moninne's family home in Co. Down, is in Ulster, in the north of Ireland. There she founded her convent at the southeast foot of the mountain, which in time became known as Killeavy, or 'Killevy' (Cell Slébe Cuilinn), 'church of the mountain'. To really understand the importance of why Monnine might have chosen Slieve Gullion Mountain, let me tell you more about the area and its important stories.

Slieve Gullion is the central 'plug' of an extinct volcano in the centre of a ring of mountains. Together they would have made one super-huge volcano! Over time, after the eruption, the runny magma that had come out from the centre of the earth cooled and collapsed back down into the ground, forming a caldera. It left a ring; a dyke of mountains around Slieve Gullion. This area is therefore called the Ring of Gullion. It is so fascinating and beautiful that scientists from all over the world travel there to study it. It is also now designated an Area of Outstanding

Natural Beauty (AONB). No doubt Moninne preached about the beauty of God's creation there. She would also have told people that God was greater than the pagan Irish gods and goddesses of mountains!

One such creator goddess associated with mountains, and especially well-known at Slieve Gullion (even before Monninne was born), was the Cailleach. She was so famous that her stories were told throughout Ireland, Scotland and the Isle of Man. There was a famous local story in Co. Armagh that said the goddess Áine and her sister Milucra (a local name of the Cailleach) both loved the legendary hero Fionn mac Cumhaill (Finn McCool). Now, there is a small lough at the top of Slieve Gullion, called Calliagh Berras Lough. Milucra, also known as the Cailleach, knew that Áine had vowed never to marry a man with grey hair. Vain goddess! So Milucra secretly put a spell on the lough so that anyone who swam in it would become old straight away! She then played a trick on Fionn. She pretended that her gold ring had fallen into its waters and asked Fionn to fetch it for her. Poor Fionn, even though he was a wise hunter and an all-round hero (as well as a giant, they say), came out of the water as an old man with grey-white hair. His men, called the Fianna, forced Milucra to give Fionn a magic potion to undo what she had done. Thankfully, Fionn became young again but his hair colour never returned! That is the story of how Fionn got his name, as in Irish 'Fionn' means 'white' (or 'fair').

So why did I tell you about Fionn and the Cailleach? Well, Moninne was born in the early fifth century, not that long after Christianity was brought to Ireland. Many people still believed the old pagan druid stories and worshipped the old Irish gods and goddesses. Well, I suggest that Moninne spent her time telling people at Killeavy that the Cailleach who they knew of so well had no power over them. The Cailleach, among her roles, was said to be the creator goddess of mountains, so Moninne would have corrected that and told people that God from the Bible alone had made them.

Another message that I believe Monnine shared was how she got *her* name. You see, not only did the famous hero Fionn mac Cumhaill (Finn McCool) get his name on Slieve Gullion, but so did the hero Cú Chulainn! As a boy, Cú Chulainn was known as Sétanta. He gained his name Cú Chulainn after having to kill a fierce guard dog guarding the home of Culann the metalsmith at Slieve Gullion. Cú Chulainn means 'Culann's hound', as once Sétanta had killed Cu-

152

lann's hound, he then promised to protect Culann's home himself. Moninne no doubt shared how she had prayed to heal the poet who couldn't speak and so received *her* name!

Cailleach, the mountain god, was also said to be a goddess of the seasons. She was said to rule over the winter months from the ancient festivals of Samhain (1st November) to Beltane/Lá Bealtaine (1st May), which marked the seasons. Even now, centuries after Monnine's life, some pilgrims who visit her holy well at Killeavy bring a rag doll, Bábóg na Bealtaine ('May-time dolly'), dressed in lace and flowers. By bringing it to a holy well, it remembers that it is God alone who is ruler over the seasons. It also might be a continued legacy Monnine told the local people that God was in charge of the seasons. Moninne would have loved this Bible verse:

It was you who set all the boundaries of the earth;
you made both summer and winter.
- Psalm 74:17, NIV

Monnine's Killeavy convent at Slieve Gullion started with eight unmarried ladies and a widow with a baby boy. The baby, called Luger, was lovingly raised by the nuns and, of course, he became a bishop! It is said Killeavy convent grew to over 150 nuns.

We know that Brigid of Kildare and Moninne kept in contact. There is a lovely story of how Brigid wanted Monnine to receive a silver drinking vessel. Monnine wouldn't accept such a special gift, so Brigid ordered it thrown into the River Liffey, which runs through Dublin. Somehow, the vessel miraculously ended up in 'Caput Litoris', which is probably Newry (just a few miles northeast of Killeavy). It must have travelled through the Irish Sea, as Newry is on the River Clanrye, which flows into Carlingford Lough. There, Moninne's brother Rónán found it. In another version of the story, Fanchea threw the vessel into the river from where she was in Co. Fermanagh. It then drifted through the river and sea currents to Monnine at Killeavy. Again, it must have travelled to Newry, and someone brought it to her!

There is also a great story about wolves at Slieve Gullion. The story goes: 'Another time, wolves suddenly came rushing from the woods and attacked the nuns' calves, which were grazing by the mountain near the convent. And they put the calves to flight and snatched one away with them.' The nuns of course told Monnine what had happened. She answered: 'Do not be distressed about this. For, He who seized the prophet Daniel safe from the jaws of the lions, will take the calf from the wolves' teeth and restore it unhurt.' She was explaining that if God protected Daniel (from the Old Testament in the Bible) from lions, then surely he would protect their calf. The story continues, 'The following day the wolves brought the untouched calf back to its pasture!'

Moninne wasn't just known for miracles, but also for her seriously strict life! She and her nuns fasted so much that it was said they were brought close to death. There is a story of some other saints visiting Killeavy to check that they were surviving the fasting. Once, twelve beautiful dresses miraculously appeared at Killeavy, but Moninne would not allow her nuns to wear them; she wanted them to be sold for the poor. At night, Moninne is also said to have stood in the cold waters of a spring and there read the whole Book of Psalms! Moninne would have had 150 psalms in her copy, which is in the Bible. That is a lot of reading, in cold water under the moonlight!

It is also said that Moninne travelled widely, as she is said to have founded seven churches in Scotland (all on mountains)! She never stopped preaching against the Cailleach. She was known in Scotland as Edin or Medena. She also went to England and possibly founded four churches, and to Rome as well! Moninne is also said to have founded churches at Swords near Dublin and Armagh.

Especially towards the end of her life, Moninne had very high standards about men. It is written that she and her nuns travelled at night to remain uncorrupted by the sight of worldly things. 'She is said never to have looked at a man, and would go out at night veiled in case she met anyone!' One of Moninne's hagiographers, who wrote a Latin Life about her, describes how she had the soul of a man in the body of a woman. She would not have liked that! What do you think the hagiographer (who lived in medieval times) meant by his description of Moninne? Did he mean something good, or bad?

Moninne lived until she was a very old lady. There is a story that friends tried to persuade her to stay on earth one extra year, but she knew once the time came that it was her time for heaven, as God had given her a vision about it. Moninne died in 517 AD:

Nine score years together
According to rule, without error,
Without folly, without evil, without danger,
Was the age of Moninne.
– Annals of the Four Masters

☞ **How many years do the Annals of the Four Masters *say Moninne lived?***

⁕ ⁕ ⁕

Moninne truly was a mighty woman of the mountains. This is how she was described in the 6th July entry in the *Martyrology of Óengus*:

Moninne of the mountain
Of Cuillin was a fair pillar:
She gained a triumph,
a hostage of purity,
A kinswoman of great Mary.

However, that was not the end of miracles at Killeavy and Slieve Gullion. At the time of the fourth abbess, Derlasre, they were building a new building at the convent and needed timber. The Abbess selected an especially large tree that was essential for part of the structure. But once cut, they found it was too heavy to move! The next day, when they came outside, what should be lying exactly where they needed it at the new building site, but the huge tree? They looked around in the forest for signs that someone had dragged it through the undergrowth, but there was nothing disturbed. Then, by chance, they looked up and saw broken branches high up by the felled tree in the canopy. It was very clear that miracles were still happening at Slieve Gullion!

You might ask, did Killeavy Church keep anything of Moninne's? Well, it is known that for centuries they kept some of her few possessions as relics. They had her comb, which she combed her hair with once a year (on Holy Thursday of Easter week)! Yes, she combed her hair just once a year. They also kept her hoe (used for gardening) and her dress made from badger skin.

And what happened to her Killeavy Church? In the decades that followed Moninne's passing, Killeavy convent was plundered by the pagan Vikings. Nevertheless, monastic life carried on in between. Later, Augustinian nuns used the site from the twelfth century until 1542, when it was closed during the reign of King Henry VIII, who shut down all the monasteries. If you go to Killeavy today, you will still see two old church buildings in ruins. One might date back to the tenth century, the other dates to the fifteenth century. There are also lots of lovely carved stones, graves, and even Moninne's grave. Also, her holy well is further up Slieve Gullion Mountain.

Going without food - Sorry I can't!

Moninne was also known for her fasting (going without food)! Many Christians still fast, especially in the six weeks of Lent from Ash Wednesday to Easter. Sometimes they only give up one food, for example, chocolate! What food(s) would you find hardest to stop eating? Pancakes are made in Ireland to use up fatty rich foods on Shrove Tuesday, the day before the start of Lent. Why don't you have a go at making pancakes with an adult?

DID YOU KNOW?

157

- ❋ Feast day: 6th July.
- ❋ Other names: Darercae, Sáirbhile, Blinne, Bline, Blathnad and Monenna (Edin and Medena in Scotland).
- ❋ The seven churches Moninne is said to have founded in Scotland are: Cilnacase, Dunbreton, Dundevenal, Stirling, Edinburgh, Dunpelder and Lanfortin.
- ❋ The Killeavy Camino is a five-hour walk, beginning at Faughart Graveyard. Walkers then travel to Killeavy Old Churches and on to St Moninne's holy well, further up Slieve Gullion.
- ❋ A piece of folklore from Oriel (a medieval kingdom in south Ulster) says that if it rains on Moninne's feast day (6th July), the bad weather will last until Lady's Day (15th August).
- ❋ The beautiful Kilnasaggart Pillar Stone is a very short distance south of Killeavy. Dating to about 700 AD, it is thought to be the oldest Christian monument in Ireland. It has a total of thirteen crosses on its two faces with an Irish inscription, which roughly translates to: 'This place, Ternoc, son of Ciaran the little, bequeath it under the protection of Apostle Peter.' It's also said to have the hoof mark of a famous cow who produced milk in amazing abundance. One day, she was milked through a sieve, which she didn't like, so kicked the stone and left the area forever!

Supernatural Samthann

Do you know what fire is a symbol of in Christianity? Well, you are about to hear the answer to that question! Let's heat things up and see if there are any blazing flames or fiery sparks in Samthann's story...

Samthann was a girl from east Co. Down, Ulster. We know that her father was called Diamrán of the Dál Fiatach, and that her mother was called Columba. It was said that Samthann was distantly related to St Patrick, who lived over 200 years before her. However, as was common at that time in Ireland (especially as it strengthened alliances between families), Samthann was fostered. Her foster-father, called Críodán, was King of Cairbre in northern Tethbae (in Co. Longford). Co. Longford is in the province of Leinster, and so Samthann and her family made the long journey southwest from Co. Down to Co. Longford.

As Samthann grew older, her foster-father the King organised for her to be married to a nobleman. But of course, Samthann, like nearly all the other saints in this book, wanted to just serve God and not marry! In fact, Samthann had a long list in her head of specific things that she would like to do in her life, and none involved getting married.

Samthann prayed for help from God, and the most amazing series of events happened. The night before the wedding, the nobleman who was her betrothed was staying at the castle. At midnight, he saw something like a ray of the sun coming through the roof! He went through the castle from room to room, looking to see where it went. Imagine his surprise when it went down into the King's daughter's bedroom. He was so fascinated by it that he became quite impertinent and brazenly opened the door, to find the ray of sun was over the girl he hoped to marry. Samthann was fast asleep beside her two foster sisters. The nobleman, so engaged

159

with what he saw, went closer and found Samthann's face lit up with the sun, in the middle of the night. He thought to himself, she must be very special!

The next day, Samthann and the nobleman were married. Perhaps it seemed too late for God to rescue her from a marriage that she didn't want... But that night, after her new husband had fallen asleep, Samthann prayed. Then, for the second night in a row, something amazing happened at midnight. Samthann looked outside, for it seemed like the sky was alight. Indeed, the town was on fire! Then it looked as if Samthann herself was on fire, from her mouth to the roof. Loud cries and shrieks could be heard from outside!

While the people tried to put out the flames, Samthann went out and hid herself in a cluster of ferns nearby. At this, an equally strange thing happened: the fire immediately disappeared without doing any damage to the town. When morning came, Samthann and her foster-father, the King, spoke together about all the strange things that had happened. Samthann explained that fire was a symbol of the Holy Spirit and that it was God communicating that she was to be allowed to be a nun, which is what she wanted instead of being married. In the end, because of the amazing events that had happened, the King and her newlywed husband both gave their permission for her to go to a convent. So off she set for the convent of Urney (Earnaidhe) in Co. Tyrone, in the northwest of Ireland, to serve God under the Abbess St Cognat.

Over time, Samthann worked tirelessly, and her positive outlook and sense of humour always shone through in her personality. Meanwhile, down in Samthann's old home of Co. Longford, the foundress of Clonbroney (Cluain Brónaig), Abbess St Fuinech, had a prophetic dream from God. Of course, knowing the story so far, we can guess it involved fire! Sure enough, St Fuinech had dreamt that sparks of fire in the likeness of Samthann filled her whole convent. She told her dream to the nuns and told them what she felt: 'Burning with the fire of the Holy Spirit, Samthann will make this place shimmer by virtue of her merits and in the splendour of miracles.' With no doubts, she passed on the leadership of Clonbroney convent to Samthann.

Samthann's community lived a simple life with only six cows. She was also known for her prayer life and performed many amazing miracles of healing, but also miracles involving food. She always showed her good humour too. She was having a new church oratory built and, unknown to everyone else, one of the workers had a secret wish. He'd been working hard and was hungry! Oh, he wished for a great feast for himself and all his co-workers of forty loaves of bread with butter and even cheese as a treat, and plenty of milk to drink. Imagine his stunned look when Samthann had that exact meal brought to them. She giggled and said to him, 'The thought of your heart is fulfilled, is it not?' As the Bible says:

> Hope deferred makes the heart sick,
> but a longing fulfilled is a tree of life.
> – Proverbs 13:12, NIV

When we want something to happen and it doesn't happen, it often makes us sad and disappointed. However, Samthann really was like a tree of life to everyone! Through her prayers, God used her to make wishes come true.

Another story hints at Samthann's sense of humour, as I think God probably worked out the funny details for her. A nearby monk fell in love with one of Clonbroney's nuns. Unfortunately for him, the poor fellow tried to meet the girl, and as he was walking across the river one day to her, a giant eel rose out of the water and bit him in his private parts! And giant eels are no laughing matter! It then wrapped itself around his waist and remained in that position until he went to the convent with all the girls able to see and begged for Samthann's forgiveness.

Samthann was also the sort of girl throughout her life who showed that not only was she loving, but that she was well able to stick up for herself. She was also extremely prophetic and often saw many events occurring with people, even at a great distance, and the thoughts of others were often revealed to her.

One day, she was having another building project completed, and they needed pine wood to build a hall. She sent one of the nuns, Nathea, with the craftsmen into the forest of Connacht to the west of them. On the first day they didn't find any timber. Day two was the same. They weren't having much luck finding it! By the third day, they were all tired and decided to come back to the convent the following day. That night, Samthann prayed and Nathea had a dream of Samthann speaking to her: 'Tomorrow morning, cut down bog willows at the root, and you will find enough pine lying there.' In the morning, they followed Samthann's instructions and found huge amounts of pine. So much so that the owner was in a foul mood and demanded payment! Nathea said they would pay willingly. The next night, of course, you can guess who Samthann appeared in a vision to. Samthann told that grumpy owner of the woods that he would soon die if he didn't do penance for his terrible behaviour! Stinging with guilt the next morning, he organised for sixty yokes of oxen to take all the wood back to the convent – a huge amount of wood!

Samthann was also full of wisdom and people flocked to her for advice. Once, a monk asked her what position he should pray in. Samthann said it is possible to pray in any position – standing, sitting or lying. Another person, a teacher, thought that they should stop reading the Bible and just pray. Samthann advised him against that! She said that the Bible is useful for helping you concentrate and reading it stops your mind from wandering. That same teacher also wanted to go on a pilgrimage to another country far away, but Samthann reminded him that God is everywhere and so you don't need to go on pilgrimage to find Him.

Even when Samthann wasn't shown respect, she had a good sense of humour about it and treated those people with kindness. For example, when she was an old lady, the monks from Iona brought her over some wool across the North Channel and Irish Sea. Iona is a small famous island in the Inner Hebrides of modern-day Scotland. A storm blew up on the way and an extremely foolish young monk said, 'Let's throw the granny's wool overboard lest we sink.' But the waves died down as soon as the navigator of the currach refused. Then, the next problem was that there was no wind, so they had to row. The boy said, 'Why can't the granny provide us any wind now?' The navigator explained that they should believe God would help them, exactly *because* the wool was going to the holy St Samthann. Upon uttering those words, the wind blew in just the right amount for three days until they reached their destination at the mouth of the River Boyne! The Iona monks kissed Samthann's hand when they arrived. When the foolish boy came near, she said: 'Now what was that you were saying about me at sea when the storm threatened you with death?' The boy was silenced with shame. In kindness, she said to him: 'Never doubt this, if ever dangers corner you, call upon me boldly.'

There is a lovely story about the night that Samthann died. It was the year 739 AD and a friend of Samthann's called Abbot Lasran woke up at the same time. He looked outside and saw not one moon, but TWO! He then looked at them both (as you would), and one of them dipped towards him! He immediately remembered a request that he had made to Samthann that, on her way to heaven, she would bow to him. He exclaimed, 'Well done, Samthann, faithful servant of God, for now you are ushered into the rejoicing of the Lord, your spouse.' The moon faded away and Lasran knew she had gone to be with her spiritual husband, Jesus, for that is what a spouse means. You see, in the Bible the church is called 'the bride of Christ'. Not only that, but as a nun Samthann had taken extra vows to be Christ's spiritual wife instead of a human wife. Samthann was now enjoying eternal life forever.

Samthann's bucket list

Samthann made a list in her head of things that she'd
like to do when she was older. Why don't you make a list
too, or draw yourself doing them on paper! For example,
travelling the world!

DID YOU KNOW?

* **Feast day:** 19th December.

* **Other names:** Samhthann, Samthana and Samthand.

* Samthann was a respected member of a group called the Céli Dé (or Culdees), which means 'companions of God'. They admired many female saints and commemorated a cluster of them. They wrote a hymn to Samthann in the margin of one of their manuscripts called *The Martyrology of Tallaght*.

* Fire is a symbol of the Holy Spirit (e.g. in Acts 2:3-4, what seemed like tongues of fire fell on the early Christians and they were filled with the Holy Spirit).

* A report in the *Annals of the Four Masters* states that a great autumn storm destroyed the monastery of Clonbroney in 783 AD.

* High King of Ireland, Áed Allán, son of Fearghal (d. 743), wrote a poem about Samthann!

* The national school in Ballinalee, Co. Longford (near Clonbroney), is named Scoil Samhthann Ballinalee.

163

Sunniva to Scandinavia

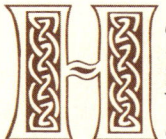 *allo og hilsen!* Hello and greetings! My name is Hallfreðr Óttarsson and I am a skáld (court poet) from Iceland who works for the kings of Norway! First I served Jarl Hákon Sigurðarson, ruler of Norway from about 975 to 995, then Olaf Tryggvason, King of Norway from 995 to 1000. Now, I serve Eiríkr Hákonarson, Earl of Lade, Governor of Norway and Earl of Northumbria. I will tell you more about those first two kings later, as its very relevant.

On the subject of names, let me just add that my nickname, Hallfreðr vandræðaskáld, which has developed over time, actually means 'Troublesome Poet', but I feel that's rather unfair! I am anything but troublesome – except, perhaps, when I like to talk about myself and my job a little too much! To my credit however, I became a God-fearing Christian, partly as a result of the story I am going to tell you. At first I was a reluctant Christian, as I loved Odin, King of the Norse gods and the religion of our Scandinavian forefathers. I wrote once:

> *...but with sorrow, for well did*
> *Viðrir's [Óðinn's] power please the poet,*
> *do I conceive hate for the first husband of*
> *Frigg [Óðinn], now I serve Christ.*

As a court poet, I usually write poetry called Hrynhenda poetry, but I felt it is rather complicated for my task in narrating this story. You will be glad that I'm just going to tell the tale in as simple a way as I can! That's enough about me and my poetry. I will be telling you the tale of this beautiful runaway Irish princess now who came to our Norwegian shores. Her name was Sunniva, which means 'sun gift'. A gift from the sun describes her perfectly, as not only did it describe her sunny

164

personality and her lovely long, buttercup-yellow hair, but how she was sent to us in Scandinavia from the heavenly Son, Christ!

The story begins with Princess Sunniva inheriting her father's kingdom in Ireland. Sunniva lived there with her brother Abban and two sisters, Borni and Marita. Everything was fine in the kingdom, until one day a pagan king invaded the realm and wanted to marry Sunniva. Some say he was from our Scandinavian shores, a Viking! It is said he was a real tyrant of a man and that he started burning homes in Ireland as soon as he arrived. Sunniva felt that she had no choice but to flee Ireland to escape from him! Three ships set off with Sunniva, her siblings and many of her followers. Yet, they had no oars or sails! The will of the Almighty and the currents brought them up the North Sea. They drifted along to the 'northern way' or 'way leading to the north', as Norway is known. It must have been terrifying. Then the soaring, white-tailed sea eagles ('Iolar Mara' in Irish), which had been flying along above them, suddenly flew away. It became increasingly clear, from the winds slapping their faces and the hugeness of the waves, that a storm was approaching fast!

It took hold as soon as they were nearing Norway. Sunniva's ship was separated from her sister Borni's, who made land first, on an island called Kinn. It had a mountain called Kinnaklova, which was a memorable landmark, as it had a deep ravine cutting through the centre of the peak. There Borni stayed with their followers who had been on that ship, and according to tradition, Borni built a church there.

Sunniva's ship and the other ship of her followers were pulled further north by the storm. Everyone was glad when they reached an island called Sellø (or Selø). They came aground to the northwest of the island at a place now known as Helmavikja or Heilagramannik ('Holy Man's Cove'). Once their ship was stranded on the shore, everyone became concerned because they knew they had reached the land of the Vikings! Vikings have a somewhat nasty reputation and were the same race of people Princess Sunniva was seeking to avoid.

Over the coming days, they explored the tiny island. It was only one mile wide. There were sheep and spring lambs grazing the grass. Sunniva stroked the little lambs, and she remembered that the Bible taught that God is our shepherd, and that He will take care of us, His sheep. Being an island, the small band of people were able to fish for food around the shores. There was also a cave on the island, where they sheltered in at night.

But it wasn't long before word got out that there was a band of strangers on Sellø. A rumour circulated among the Norwegian neighbours on the mainland that surely Sunniva and her people must be killing and eating the sheep. Their livelihoods were in danger! However, Sunniva and those with her had not killed any of the sheep. But the sheep farmers didn't know that, and complained to Jarl Hákon Sigurðarson. Now, Jarl Hákon, the first king I served, was also called Hákon the Powerful (Hákon jarl hinn ríki). But he was also nicknamed Hákon Bad (Hákon Illi). Hákon the Bad was a better name for him! He was a strong believer in the old Norse gods and very against the spread of Christianity into Norway. There was nothing gracious or forgiving about him! When he heard the rumours, he headed to Sellø with his warrior army.

Sunniva and her people saw the ships full of Viking soldiers arriving from the distance. Praying and running, they fled up the forty steps to the cave. Now, Sunniva knew her Bible:

> For God so loved the world that he gave his one and only Son,
> that whoever believes in him shall not perish but have eternal life
> – John 3:16, NIV

Sunniva knew that no matter what, because she was a Christian, that even though her body would die, she would go to heaven and have eternal life. So, not fearing death, she cried out to God, 'Give our souls everlasting rest, and let Your angels break down the mountain and bury us under it!' You see, Sunniva knew the fate that waited for them once the Norsemen soldiers reached them. Surely, they would be put to death or worse. As soon as Sunniva prayed, the cave collapsed in on them and immediately they were in heaven. Jarl Hákon the Bad's men searched the whole island, but could find no one. What a mystery!

Not long after Jarl Hákon the Bad died, a Christian king came to power in Norway. He was called Olaf Tryggvason, the second king I served. Strange and unexplained things started to happen on the island. Two farmers, Tord Eigileivsson and Tord Jorunsson, anchored on the island to spend the night on a journey to Trondheim (on the mainland). They said they saw a supernatural light over the island and discovered a bleached skull with a sweet smell. It was such an unusual experience that they went to Trondheim to tell King Olaf Tryggvason and Bishop Sigurd everything that they had seen!

Then there was a similar story by someone else, so King Olaf and the Bishop travelled to Sellø and found lots of bones! But they weren't like normal bones, they all had a sweet smell coming from them. They lifted away the many rocks that had fallen down into the cave and recovered the body of St Sunniva. It looked as if she were just sleeping! Her long golden hair still fell beautifully down past her shoulders. They collected all the bones and placed them in a casket. Sunniva's body was placed in a timber shrine. They knew there was something very special about her.

King Olaf Tryggvason had a wooden church built on the island to house the bodies of Sunniva and her companions (the Seljumannamesse). Over time, the church was painted white so that people on the sea could see it. Many people started to visit the island; it became a great centre of pilgrimage. The island is so important that it was renamed Selja ('blessed/holy island').

Now, as I said, my day job is to write poetry in 'Hrynhenda', which is supposed to have eight syllables per line and two alliterations in the odd-numbered lines. But that's just the narrow definition of my usual poetry! This is a short eight syllable poem:

Sunniva, Sunniva Eire's saint
Gift from the sun, she came to shine
Three boats to Norway west they came
Son's gift with Seljumannamesse

Praise be to the beautiful Princess Sunniva! Tusen takk (thousand thanks) for reading my story! Ha det! Vi ses! Bye! See you later (as I hope you read this story many times).

❖ ❖ ❖

So, what became of Selja Island? Well, a Benedictine Abbey was built on Selja at around 1100. Sunniva's relics were moved to Christ Church in Bergen (Bjørgvin) in 1170 and as a result, many more people in Norway heard about Sunniva. Famously, there were fires in Bergen in 1170-1171 and 1198. The relics of Sunniva were taken from the cathedral and set down at Sandbru. Amazingly though, the fire halted and it seemed that a miracle took place!

Sadly, during the reformation, Sunniva's shrine was moved and then lost when Munkeliv monastery was destroyed in 1536. As far as Selja goes, monks lived there until Black Death hit in 1349, although there might have been a community there as late as 1451. However, even today Selja is a place of pilgrimage for thousands of people each year. The island is just a fifteen-minute journey by boat from the Stadlandet peninsula on the mainland. If you visit from May to September, you can book a boat from the mainland. Many of them include guided tours of Selja island and the monastery. As soon as you arrive at the harbour, you are greeted by a tall, white marble statue of Sunniva holding a rock from the cave.

Every year on the first Sunday in July, the local deanery now celebrates the Seljumannamesse (St Sunniva and her companions). There is a procession led by a girl in a white robe, representing St Sunniva, and a dozen (12) male participants wearing monks' habits.

Selja's spring water is said to be healing. Water is often taken home from it for a child's baptism, especially if the child is going to be called Sunniva! As a mark of respect, some crawl on their knees up the forty steps that lead up to the cave. Some light candles in the cave, which is dedicated to the Archangel Michael. Selja truly is a 'blessed/holy island'! Visitor's today still comment on its ancient and holy atmosphere. Today, St Sunniva is also the patron saint of the Norwegian Diocese of Bergen (Bjørgvin), as well as all of Western Norway. Every year there is still a Sunniva Festival in Bergen.

˙SUNNIVA˙

Song lyrics by Hanne Krogh. Translated from Norwegian.

It's starlight heaven.
The sea is black.
Boats glide silently from Eire.
They have no
sails, no oar, no maps.
But Sunniva sings.
The boats are rocking.
The princess asks the men to celebrate.

She no
longer knows what
she was leaving, doesn't know where they want to beach.
What sacrifices
will fate and the future take?
The thoughts
weigh, but
Sunniva sings as the boats glide through the water.

Sunniva, Sunniva,
trust your courage!
The light from Selja will shine.
And if you lift your
eyes from what you left behind, you'll never go blind.
The light from Selja will shine.

Yet the
sea and
sky can turn black without a comforting star.
For a girl, life
can still be hard.
But, Sunniva, cling
to the mast,
and sing yourself a sparkling pot in the distance.

Sunniva, Sunniva,
believe in your faith!
The light from Selja will shine.
And if you lift your
eyes from what you left behind, you'll never go blind.
The light from Selja will shine.

For the Irish
princess and you, little woman,
the light from Selja will shine.

Sunniva had a little lamb...

Make a collage picture. Use cotton wool to create the sheep
and lambs! If you are completing it in school, your teacher
could give your class yellow wool for Sunniva's long hair,
and googlie eyes for the sheep and lambs!

DID YOU KNOW?

❧ Feast days: 8th July (main) & 7th September (transportation of her body to Bergen in 1170).

❧ Other names: Summina, Summiva, Sumniva, Sunifa, Sunifra, Suniva, Sinevo, Sinney, Sommine and Sonneva.

❧ St Sunniva School is in Oslo, Norway.

❧ The *SS St Sunniva* was one of the first purpose-built cruise ships (launched in 1887). There was also a ferry from P&O Scottish Ferries in Scotland called *St Sunniva*. There have been several Norwegian ships named Sunniva.

❧ There is a St Sunniva Street in Lerwick.

❧ There is St Sunniva tea too!

❧ Nobel Prize-winning Norwegian-Danish author, Sigrid Undset, visited the remains of Selja monastery in 1926 and was inspired to write a novella based on Sunniva's story. She commissioned fifteen beautiful watercoloured illustrations for it. They were painted by her friend Gøsta af Geijerstam. One of them is a haunting portrayal of Sunniva's three ships on their way from Ireland to Norway.

171

Super Sisters

Early one morning, three young sisters were just getting up from their beds. It was really still night and not yet dawn. They each set about their day in the dim light of the moon, with the hope of the sun in the far distance. Little did they know that years from now, when they were older, their same daily morning routine would be interrupted, in a very special way. The three girls lived in the village of Cullen, in the northwest of what is now Co. Cork, in the barony of Dunhallow. Co. Cork is in the province of Munster, in the south of Ireland. There is a story that their family had originally lived in England but then moved to Ireland. The names of the three girls are as follows:

Lassar, named for the Old Irish word for 'flame' or 'fire'. It was a popular name, especially for Christian families, as the Holy Spirit descended like fire at Pentecost! It was the most popular name for female saints. There are over a dozen saints in the Irish martyrologies named versions of Lassar – Lassar, Lasra, Lassera, Lassara and Lassair; all had the same meaning. Lassar was a fiery girl with a prophetic spirit!

Next was Inneen. Inneen you might think had an unusual name, as it came from the Irish word for daughter ('iníon'). It sounds strange to modern ears perhaps. You can just imagine her parents calling her name and it always meaning 'daughter'. 'Daughter, do this!'; 'Daughter, do that!' But it was her name. Her more common name though was her nickname. She was lovingly called Inghen Buidhe. This meant 'yellow-haired daughter'. She had the loveliest golden-blonde hair. Her parents were very proud of her, as they were of all their three daughters.

Third, there was Lateerin (or 'Laitairian', as it was sometimes spelt). She was the youngest. We don't know anything about Lateerin's name, but we do know that she was very pretty and that she had the power to make curses come true! There is a story that one morning (as she always did), she was going to the blacksmith to

173

collect the 'seed' for the fire; that is, the red-hot embers to start it. Now, miracles always happened with Lateerin. She would carry the embers in her apron and it would never set fire! But one day, she scooped the embers into her apron and as she did her apron and skirt lifted a little, showing off some of her ankles and feet. The blacksmith remarked on how pretty she was. She looked down and glanced at her ankles, and was burnt by the coals as she had felt the sin of pride! My goodness, did Lateerin curse that blacksmith for what he had said. There has never been a blacksmith's forge in Cullen since, nor ever will there be, or so it is said! Neither can there be a forge within a mile of Cullen, or else the fire won't light in it. There is also a legend that after this, Lateerin disappeared down through the ground and ended up in the place where she would have a church in Cullen. The spot where she entered the ground is marked by a heart shaped stone. However, others say that this stone marks her grave.

The girls also had two brothers. One was named John, who we know started a church. Their other more famous brother was called Berechert. He founded the monastery at Tullylease, in Co. Cork, not too far from Cullen. At Tullylease, there is an eighth-century inscribed cross-slab dedicated to St Berechert, and also a holy well dedicated to him. It is said that the father of this family was a chieftain called Bhuide, but we don't know anything about their mother, except that she raised five super saintly children!

When the three girls grew up, they all knew that they wanted to start churches just like their brothers, John and Berechert. However, they wanted to keep in touch with each other, so didn't want to be that far apart. So, two of them journeyed a distance within Dunhallow and set up their churches in what would become three neighbouring parishes. Lassar went to Killasseragh townland in Kilmeen parish (northwest of Cullen); Inneen went to Dromtarriff (east of Cullen); and Lateerin stayed at home, in Cullen (since Lateerin was the youngest, her parents and the others wanted her to stay local). The three sisters were very close-knit in heart and adored seeing each other as often as they could. They worked hard to spread the good news about Jesus to each of their parishes in Dunhallow. But oh, how they missed each other and wished that it was easier to travel between their churches! You see, there were no roads between the three sites. Only fields, hedges and ditches.

But one morning, in each of their churches, Lassar, Inneen and Lateerin were just getting up from their beds, just as at the beginning of our story. Again, it was still half night and not yet dawn. They each started to set about their day in the dim light of the moon when, suddenly, an angel appeared before each of them! Three angels. One in Kilmeen, one in Dromtarriff, and one in Cullen. Each angel beckoned for them to follow behind. And what an amazing sight it was that happened! The angels said to the girls, 'Even the cows have roads in Ireland so the Lord says that you too shall have a road, that joins your three churches, so that you can visit each other more easily once a week.'

The angels lifted Inneen and Lateerin into the air to join Lassar at Kilmeen, and together the three angels and girls journeyed for miles through the still night air. Then they flew from Kilmeen about 7 miles (11.27 km) southeast to Dromtarriff. Then back west, about 9 miles (14.48 km) to Cullen! All along the way, the angels in seconds laid down a road to walk upon, where there were once just fields. What was grass turned into stone. What were hedges that formerly had to be climbed through, disappeared! That is how a narrow road, the width of two cows (called a 'cow path', or 'bóthar' in Irish), was made for three saintly sisters.

It certainly gave a new meaning to this Bible verse:

Trust in the Lord with all your heart
    and lean not on your own understanding;
in all your ways submit to him,
    and he will make your paths straight.
– Proverbs 3:5, NIV

Even today the three super sisters are remembered in Co. Cork. Lassar's well has been ploughed over, but those of the other two sisters are still visited.

There are stories about Inneen's Well at Dromtarriff. At a certain period in time, the landlords at Dromtarriff were not happy with people visiting the well. They went so far as to actually drain the Blackwater river up to it, to try to stop people visiting the well. Their thought was: no water, no visitors on their land! Now at that time, people went to the well on different occasions during the year; there was no special day of pilgrimage. The landlords also ploughed the land so that the well couldn't be seen and planted corn all over it and the surrounding area. Come 6th May, first thing in the morning, what should happen but the spring in the well bursting up through the ground? Water poured out and out, flowing up and over

SUPER SISTERS

to form a little lake (4 or 5 ft deep and a few feet wide). All the local people talked and talked about it. No one remembered the well being there before that day, as it had been gone some time. From then on, it was remembered that St Inneen's feast day was 6th May.

In another version of that story, the landlord set men to work filling in the well. The very first day, all those men got sore eyes. Some had the sense to give up and not interfere with a holy well, but some still continued (perhaps for a day's pay), and what should happen? They were turned stone blind! The story ends that the landlord saw the error of his ways and got his men who could see to repair the damage done. They built a wall around it and the owner put a man in charge of it to guard it, making sure it (and others) were kept safe. Three stones with crosses were put at the well and the tradition is to drink the water and tie a rag on the near-by hawthorn tree. The water is said to be particularly good at healing eye ailments, and men's problems.

Lateerin's well is beehive-shaped. In 1894, it is reported that a girl who was paralysed was healed and left her crutches behind at the well. There was once said to have been a golden trout in it once, which brought good luck!

176

A miraculous trip

TASK:

If you could be taken on a miraculous trip by angels, where
would you like to go? It could be anywhere in the world!
Think about any place, in any country. Why would you like
to visit that place?

DID YOU KNOW?

❀ **Feast Days:**
  - Lassar: 7th May
  - Inneen: 6th May
  - Lateerin: 25th July

❀ We don't know much about their brother John. There are three holy wells dedicated to him close by in the Mushera mountain area. His feast day is 24th June. It is said that he also had protection against fire, like his sister Lateerin.

❀ A cow road ('bóthar' in Irish) was one of the five types of road identified in medieval Irish legal texts. The others were a slige (where two chariots could pass), rót (where one chariot and two riders could pass), lámraite (two major roads connected) and tógraite (a road that led to a forest or river).

❀ Some believe that the three sisters lived earlier in history. However, that would probably mean that St Berechert at least was not their brother.

Wonder Women

It is hard to give an exact percentage of the number of Irish female saints, as sometimes names are shared by males and females. However, Dr. Elva Johnston says that females made up about 12 per cent of saints in the medieval Irish martyrologies. That is at least 240 names! As I have also written about Irish saints who are not mentioned in the Irish martyrologies, my list below is even longer - 343 names. However, there are far more than 343 saints, as many female saints shared the same name. Some saints had more than one name! They are all listed here as they were all such extraordinary 'wonder women' that they were designated saints. Please, forgive me if I have left out any that you know from your local area. Perhaps you share a name with an Irish female saint? Have a look!

- Áedammair
- Áednat
- Afraic
- Agna/Aghna
- Aighleann/Aiglenn
- Airmer
- Aithneann
- Aldetrude (might be second generation Irish)
- Althea/Alea/Athea/Atea
- Amphitina/Anpthin
- Ana
- Angas/Angais/Anghais
- Aodhamair
- Attracta/Attracht/Athracht/Araght/Atty/Arata/Tarachta/Tarahata
- Banbnat
- Barrán
- Beagnad/Begnet
- Becga/Bega
- Bega/Bee/Beya/Begh

- Begnet/Begneta/Begnete/Begnait/Becnait
- Béibhil
- Beoín
- Bicsech/Bigsech/Bigseach/Bigesg/Bicsecha
- Bimtach
- Bíthe
- Bláth/Blathnait/Flora
- Boga/Bogha
- Boing
- Breage/Breaca
- Breccnat/Breacnat
- Bríg/Brígh
- Briga
- Brigid/Brigit/Bridget/Brighid/Brid/Bride/Bríga/Brigitte/Bridie/Bree/Brídín/Biddy/Breeda
- Britta
- Broineach
- Broinnfhinn

- Brónach/Bronagh
- Bruinsech/Brunsecha
- Buriana/Berriona/Beriana/Beryan/Buryan
- Caemhog/Caemoca/Cáemóc
- Cáemnat
- Caineach
- Cainer/Canir/Cainnear/Cannera/Canair/Conainne/Canaire/Connera/Kinnera/Cainder
- Cainne
- Caírech/Caoireach
- Caisín/Caissín
- Caoimheall
- Caol
- Caolainn
- Caomhóg
- Céirseach
- Carilla
- Cera/Chera/Chier/Ciara/

Cyra/Keira/Keara/Kiara/
Kiera/Ceara/Cier/Ciar
- Ciannat
- Cíar/Ceara/Cior/Cyra/
Cera
- Cinne/Cinnia/Cynnia
- Clothru
- Cobba/Coppa
- Cóch
- Cócha/Cota/Cocca/Coca/
Coecha
- Cóel
- Cóelfind/Caoilfionn/Ca-
ellainn
- Cóemnat
- Cóemse
- Coga
- Cognat/Cognad
- Coib
- Coic
- Coimhgheall
- Coincheann
- Caoincheas
- Coíne/Coéme
- Coip/Coipp
- Caoircseach
- Coireall
- Colla
- Colma/Columba
- Colmha
- Colum
- Columb
- Columba
- Comaig/Comaigh/Com-
maig
- Comgall
- Comgell
- Comnaid/Commaneth
- Comnat
- Conac

- Conchend/Conchenna/
Coincheand
- Conna
- Connadh
- Corb
- Corcair
- Cormac/Crón
- Corpnat/Cráebnat
- Cránaid
- Cranat/Cránaid/Cran-
nat/Cranit/Craebhnat/
Craobhnad/Crawnat
- Craobh
- Craobhnad
- Craoi
- Créadh
- Créadhnad
- Criadha
- Críoda/Críod
- Crón/Cróne/Cróine/Cro-
ne/Cronia/Cronae
- Crónsech/ Crónseach
- Crotha
- Cruimhthiris
- Cuach
- Cuachnat
- Cuman/Cumman/Coman/
Inghean/Fíonmhaith
- Cuman Becc/Cumman
Beg
- Cummain/Cuman
- Cummen
- Curcach
- Dahalin/Daithlionn/Daith-
leann/Dathalan/Dahillan/
Daithle
- Dáire/Dario/Dair/Dar/
Dear/Deir
- Dairi/Daria
- Dairneassa

- Dairtinne
- Damnat/Damhnat/Damh-
nad
- Damhradh
- Dar Bellin
- Dar Erca/Dairearca
- Dar Inill
- Dar Luga
- Dar Lugdach/Darlugh-
dhach/Derlugdacha
- Darbiled/Deirbhle/
Dairbhile/Deirbhileadh/
Dirbhileadh/Dervla/Der-
vila/Derbiled/Dervilla/
Derrivla
- Darchaorthainn
- Darenia
- Dealbhnad
- Dearbhfhraoich
- Dearbhinill/Dairbhil/Dar-
belinn
- Dearinill
- Dearmhór
- Degitge/Deghitche/De-
ghitghi
- Deichtear
- Deimhlir
- Deineath
- Deirbhinill
- Déirdre
- Deirinill
- Der Chaírthinn
- Dermór/Dermoria
- Dida
- Digde/Díghe
- Díodhnad
- Díognad
- Díona/Díne
- Dominica/Drusa
- Doroma

179

- Druiden
- Druighean
- Duinseach
- Duistric
- Dúthracht
- Dymphna/Dympna
- Éadaoin
- Eche/Eiche/Echi
- Échtach
- Eglinna
- Eistean
- Eithne
- Erc/Earc
- Ercnat
- Erednat
- Erníne/Earanain/Earnan
- Étaín/Edania/Edana/Edoena/Etaoin/Etavin/Eidin/Héidin
- Ethne/Eithne/Ethnea/Ethna
- Faber/Fedbair/Feadhbhair/Fionnbharr/Fiadhabhair
- Facundide
- Faílend
- Failtigern/Faoiltigern
- Fanchea/Fuinche/Fainche/Fuinchea/Fainc/Funchea/Faine
- Faoileann
- Fearga
- Fedelm/Feidhealm
- Femme/Feime
- Femmor
- Fiadnat/Fiadhnat
- Fiamhain
- Fidelma/Fidelmia
- Fínchell/Finncheall
- Finneach
- Findche
- Findsech
- Fine/Finia
- Fintína/Finntina
- Fiona
- Fionmhaith
- Fionn
- Flann
- Flannaid
- Fled/Fledh
- Foílenn/Foila/Faile/Foilenna
- Forbhaise
- Fordeoir/Foirdeoir
- Francla
- Fraonchnad
- Fuineacht
- Fuinech
- Gabthene
- Geilghéis
- Gema/Gemma
- Gobnait/Gobnaid/Gobnad/ Abigail/Deborah
- Golinia/Golina
- Gontrude (might be French?)
- Grimonia/Grimonie
- Gubsech
- Helena
- Hieu
- Ia/Hya/Hia/Eia
- Iamhnad
- Imy/Ibie/Imer/Iomar/Iomhar
- Indecht
- Inghean/Ingheana
- Inne
- Inneen/Inghen Buidhe
- Íte/Íde/Ita/Mida/Ida/Ides/Deirdre
- Lallóg
- Lann
- Lassair/Lasar/Lassar/Lasra/Lassera/Laisre/Lassara
- Lateerin/Laitairian
- Lazar
- Lelia
- Lí Ban/Liban/Líobhan/Fuinche/Muirgein/Muirgeilt
- Liadhain/Liadán/Liedania
- Liamhain/Liamain
- Libaria/Libaire (might be French?)
- Líobha
- Líth
- Lochina/Lóichín
- Luadrenn
- Luiceall/Luicill
- Luidhean
- Luaithrenn/Luaithrinn
- Luchair
- Luiceall
- Luidhean/Luiden
- Luigsech/Laoighseach
- Lúit/Lutt
- Lupait/Lubaid/Lupita
- Macha
- Machain
- Madelberte (might be second generation Irish)
- Mærwynn/Merewenna/Merwinna
- Maghna
- Maithgheim
- Masse/Maisse
- Maura
- Maxentia/Maxence
- Mayoca/Mazota
- Meall

- Mealla
- Medan
- Medb/Meadhbh
- Meithean
- Mella
- Menna/Menne (might be French?)
- Metán/Meattan
- Methel
- Miadnat/Midabaria/Miodhabhair
- Míanach
- Mica/Míca/Micca
- Míoda
- Miodhan
- Mo Cholla/Mocholla
- Mo Chonna/Mo Cenna/Mocheanna
- Mo Chua
- Mo Manna/Momhanna
- Mo Ninne
- Mo Theca/Teca
- Mochaomhra
- Modwenna/Modwen
- Mogain
- Moingfhinn
- Moinis
- Monessa
- Moninne/Darercae/Sáirbhile/Blinne/Bline/Blathnad/Monenna/Edin/Medena
- Muadnat
- Mugain/Mughain/Mogain
- Náire
- Naomhaidhe
- Neamhnad
- Neas/Cneas
- Neimheadh
- Ode (might be French?)
- Odarnat
- Odhbha
- Osmanna/Osmana/A-gariarga
- Osnat/Osnad
- Pandionia/Pandwyna
- Piala/Phiala
- Pompa
- Portia
- Promptia
- Proof/Preuve/Santa Froba
- Rathnat
- Rechtíne
- Richell/Rícheall/Ríceann
- Rígnach/Ríoghnach
- Rímhtheach
- Ríomh
- Rónaid
- Rose
- Ruadhnad
- Ruithche
- Samthann/Samhthann/Samthana/Samthand
- Sanct Bhróg
- Saorlaith
- Sárbile
- Sárnat/Sárnad/Sárnat/Sórnach/Surney/Sourney
- Scanlach/Scannlach
- Scíath
- Scíre
- Scoth
- Searc
- Sicilde/Sicildis/Séraute/Cérotte/Sichildis/Aclythenis
- Sinche
- Sinech/Sineach
- Sineall
- Síon
- Sodelb
- Soghaois
- Soibhean
- Soidhealbh
- Sorbhlaith
- Sporóc/Sproc
- Suaibsech/Suibhsech/Suabseg
- Sunniva/Summina/Summiva/Sumniva/Sunifa/Sunifra/Suniva/Sinevo/Sinney/Sommine/ Sonneva
- Susanna/Suzanne (might be French?)
- Syra/Syre
- Táimthene
- Teamhair
- Tecla (might be Welsh?)
- Tighearn
- Tigris
- Tiu/Tua/Thiu
- Tochomracht/Tochumra
- Tochumra
- Trea
- Tréidhe
- Tuililatha/Tuilelaith/Tallulla/Tulilach/Tuilclath
- Uaininn

Below are descriptions of some female saints I didn't have enough information about to write a long story on, but who are still interesting!

⊗ Cera/Chera/Chier/Ciara/Cyra/Keira/Keara/Kiara/Kiera/Ceara/Cier/Ciar

One day there was a serious fire. St Brendan instructed the people to pray to Cera. Cera prayed, and it was miraculously put out! However, details about her life might be mixed up a little, as there were probably two saints called Cera (hence so many potential feast days). She either lived in the sixth or seventh century. She might have lived to a very old age. Feast days: 5th January, 15th March, 2nd July and 15th December.

⊗ Coca/Cuaca

Did you know that there was a saint with the same name as a famous soft drink? Coca was the sixth-century founder of Cill Choca, 'Coca's Church' in Kilcock, Co. Kildare. She was said to have been a sister of St Kevin of Glendalough. By occupation, she was an embroiderer of church vestments, including those for St Columba/Colmcille, a very famous monk who lived on Iona! The Catholic church in Kilcock is called St Coca's. Feast days: 8th January and 6th June.

⊗ Cócha/Cota/Cocca/Coca/Coecha

Cócha was Abbess of Ross Bennchuir, near where the River Fergus joins the River Shannon in Co. Clare. It is close to Quin Abbey. She lived in the fifth century and is known for two things. Firstly, she was Ciarán of Saigir's nurse. Secondly, she is known for her ploughing. St Ciarán would send her his oxen to plough with and they never got lost on the way! Feast day: 29th June.

⊗ Cuman/Cumman/Coman/Inghean Bhaoith/Fionmhaith

This famous motherly saint has been mentioned several times throughout the book. Cuman either had 20 or 47 children! The reason there are two such different numbers is because scholars have two different sources. The *Book of Lismore* says she had twenty, but *The Tract on the Mothers of the Saints* says she had 47 – and that 45 of those were saints! The story is that her womb was blessed by St Patrick. Sadly, there is no family tree for me to draw for you to show all her children. However, we do know many of their names and where their churches were. She had both sons and daughters. Like some other saints, she has more than one name. We also know that she was associated with a church in Leinster and perhaps Killinaboy, Co. Clare. She was also an aunt of St Brigid of Kildare. Professor Emeritus Pádraig Ó Riain, who is an expert on Irish saints (especially the *Tract on the Mothers of the Saints*), wrote that she got the name Cuman from her father, as he used the term comain/comaoin ('favour') when speaking to her. Feast days: possibly 29th December and 5th or 6th May.

◈ Cummen

This economically shrewd saint made wise money decisions!

The Book of Armagh tells the story of Cummen, a nun who used what would have been her dowry to buy half an estate in Armagh. She later bought out the other half through clever trading. We're told she made an elaborate mantle and sold it for a brown horse which, in turn, she sold for a cumal of silver, equivalent in value to three cows.' Clodagh Finn, *Through Her Eyes: A New History of Ireland in 21 Women*. Feast day: unknown.

◈ Dáire/Dario

There was a nun called Dáire who was a member of St Brigid of Kildare's monastery. There is a story that one evening St Brigid sat with Dáire as the sun was going down. It was a beautiful sunset, as all sunsets are, yet Dáire was blind, so could not see it. They were busy talking so much about Christ and heaven that before they knew it, it was morning already. They had chatted all night! Where they sat, Brigid could see the sun coming up from the Wicklow mountains. Again, earth was so beautiful; bathed in the light of dawn. Brigid sighed, for she saw how lovely everything looked and knew that Dáire couldn't see any of it. The story continues that Brigid bowed her head and prayed before extending her hand and making the sign of the cross on Dáire's eyes. Immediately, Dáire could see! She saw the 'golden ball in the east, while all the trees and flowers glittered with dew in the morning light'. Dáire looked a little while and then, turning to Brigid, said: 'Close my eyes again, dear mother, for when the world is so visible to the eyes, God is seen less clearly to the soul.' So Brigid prayed once more, and Dáire's eyes 'grew dark again'. Feast day: possibly 8th August.

Dar Lugdach/Darlughdhach/Derlugdacha

Dar Lugdach was St Brigid of Kildare's favourite pupil and her successor. There is a great story where she was once tempted to meet with a suitor. To stop herself from meeting him, she put burning coals in her shoes! The next morning, Brigid prayed for her feet and they were healed. She is said to have died one year to the day after St Brigid died, and they share the same feast day. Feast day: 1st February.

Dominica/Drusa

She was the sister of the more famous saint, St Indracht, an Irish prince. They lived in either the seventh-eighth or ninth century. We know that they were on a pilgrimage to Rome when they were murdered by Saxon brigands (highway robbers). Historically, Dominia is only mentioned in a later version of the story, along with miracles that were said to have happened. It's also possible that her brother was an Iona abbot. Their relics are at Glastonbury in England. Feast days: 5th February and 8th May.

Eithne & Fedelm

These two were daughters of the King of Tara. They were baptised by St Patrick. They wanted to see God so much that it was recorded that they died straight away! There is also a similar story for the British princess, St Ness/Munessa, who was also baptised by St Patrick, near Armagh, and died straight away after baptism. Feast day: 11th January.

Étaín/Edania/Edana/Edoena/Etaoin/Etavin/Eidin/Héidin

Étaín was based at Tumna (Tuaim Nóa), 'the tomb of the woman', Co. Roscommon, near where the River Boyle and River Shannon join. There is a holy well there bearing her name, and prayers stones. She is known for giving her name to Lough Eidin (though it is also known as Lough Drumharlow). Feast day: 5th July.

◈ Flannaid

We know that Flannaid was an Irish princess from Fermoy, Co. Cork. There is a story that St Carthach/Mo Chutu (d. 639) of Lismore was travelling in the area when he found an apple near the River Blackwater. Flannaid at the time was lame in one arm (she couldn't use it), but St Carthach/Mo Chutu used the apple to heal her! No more details of the story are known. Flannaid went on to become a nun and founded a church at Clondulane, in the barony of Condons and Clangibbon, Co. Cork. Feast day: unknown.

◈ Fordeoir/Foirdeoir

Fordeoir was a maternal sister of St Aighile, Abbot of Clonmacnoise in Co. Offaly (they had the same mother). There is a story that her brother, Aighile, got on the wrong side of Diarmuid (d. 833), King of Connacht, so the King tried to have Aighile removed from his job as abbot! Aighile turned to his sister, Fordeoir, who was a nun, for help. She placed a curse on King Diarmuid and his descendants (except a child still in the womb) that deprived them of kingship. Feast day: unknown.

◈ Hieu

Hieu lived in the seventh century. She founded abbeys at Hartlepool in Co. Durham, and Healaugh near Tadcaster, Yorkshire, England. She was appointed by St Aidan of Lindisfarne. It is said that she was the first abbess in England to rule over a double monastery with both men and women. An important job! Feast day: 2nd September.

◈ Kentigerna/Caintigern

Kentigerna lived in the seventh and eighth century, first in Ireland and then in Scotland. Her father was Cellach Cualann, King or Prince of Leinster. Sadly, her husband died, so with her brother St Comgan, her son St Fillan and her two other children, she went to Scotland. They also had seven other companions with them. Eventually, Kentigerna lived as a hermit at what is now called Strath Fillan, on the island of Inchcailloch in Loch Lomond. The name of that island means, 'island of the old woman'. She died in the year 733 or 734 and was buried on Inchcailloch. Feast day: 7th January.

◈ Large Groupings

23rd February is the feast of the twelve daughters of Óengus mac Nad Froích, the legendary fifth-century King of Cashel and Munster. He was converted by St Patrick. Óengus, King of Cashel, gave twelve daughters and twelve sons to the Church, still leaving him twelve more sons and twelve daughters!

11th August is the day in the Irish martyrology calendar where there are the most female saints celebrated than any other day. These are five named female saints and 3 sets of sisters! Banbnat, Indecht, Liadain, Míanach, Attracta, and the daughters of Senach, of Dutu, and of Donnán.

◈ Mazota/Mayoca

Mazota was a fifth- to sixth-century virgin who led a group of nine holy maidens to join St Brigid on a visit to Pictland (modern day Scotland), which led to the founding of a church at Abernethy (Aburnethige). She is also associated with Drumoak (Dalmaik), Aberdeenshire. Feast day: 23rd December.

◈ Medan

Medan went to Scotland and lived in Galloway in the eighth century. St Medan's Cave & Chapel can still be seen in Kirkmaiden, Wigtownshire. There is a story that she and her nuns travelled across Luce Bay using a rock as a boat! Feast day: 19th November.

◈ Modwenna/Modwen

Modwenna lived in the seventh century. We know that she was a noblewoman, and that she founded Burton Abbey, Staffordshire, in England. She spent seven years there with two other Irish nuns, Lazar and Althea. She went on a pilgrimage to Rome, then built a church at Stapenhill for saints Peter and Paul. Later, she travelled to Scotland and died near Dundee when she was 130 years old! The local Church of England in Burton upon Trent is called St Modwen's after her. The local Roman Catholic church is called SS Mary and Modwen's. A traditional story tells that on her death, her companions saw her soul taken to heaven by silver swans, which became her emblem. The swan is remembered by the large white swan sculpture in Stapenhill Gardens. It is also said that it was Modwenna who first brought mute swans to the area. Feast day: 5th July.

✦ Mugain/Mughain/Mogain

Mugain of Clogher, Co. Tyrone, lived in the sixth century. One day, she fell and unfortunately broke her hip! She prayed and it is said she invoked the name of St Columba/Colmcille of Iona. We know from St Adomnán, who wrote about it, that when St Columba heard of her plight and prayer, he sent a messenger with a cure. He also sent a promise of twenty-three more years of good work. Feast day: unknown.

✦ Mums

Some of the Irish female saints remained unmarried throughout their lives, while others are mothers (including some mothers of very famous male saints).

✦ Tochomracht/Tochumra

Tochomracht was based with the Conmaicne, a group of peoples in Connacht, who gave their name to Connemara according to Dr. Elva Johnston. This saint is said to have been called on by women in labour, in Kilmore, Co. Cavan. Feast day: 11th June.

✦ Unnamed

There is the fascinating story of a sixth-century holy woman whose name is unknown, but St Columba/Colmcille of Iona in Scotland saw her borne into heaven by angels!

Quiz

1. Who is especially known for taming many animals?

2. Who stood on a leaf as it turned into a boat, which then carried her across the Irish and Celtic Seas?

3. Who was told to start a church at the place where she saw nine white deer?

4. Who is known for her work with linen?

5. How did Fanchea get her nickname in Irish (Fuinche 'garb')?

6. Who put a curse on the Sillees River in Co. Fermanagh?

7. What is the Norwegian word for a court poet?

8. What is a currach?

9. Who chose to stay blind so that she could focus on God more?

10. A monk fell in love with one of St Samthann's nuns. What happened to the poor monk?

11. Where did Vincent van Gogh's father consider sending him (to treat his mental illness)?

12. What are the two promises if you can squeeze through the window of St Darbiled's church ruins in Co. Mayo?

13. Who blinded some pirates to protect herself?

14. Who walked on water to Scattery Island, Co. Clare?

15. Who wrote, 'The blood of the martyrs is the seed of the church'?

16. What were Sunniva and her followers accused of doing?

17. Who lived for about 300 years?

18. Where was Brigid the Younger taken to by angels?

19. Who had either 20 or 47 children?

20. How many Irish female saints have Latin Lives written about them?

21. Who is described as 'foster-mother of the saints'?

22. Who rung her bell to warn sailors of danger when the lough beside her church was stormy?

23. Who is known for an especially 'fiery' life?

24. Whose name means 'sun gift'?

25. A scary serpent was one of the monstrous creatures that St Attracta killed. In the legend, what became of its eggs?

26. Who was given a lovely bracelet by an angel?

27. Whose cloak became like a hard board so she and her nuns could sail across the sea on it, after visiting her brother, St Énda of Aran?

28. Who survived being locked up in prison, a storm at sea, and went to Gaul (now called France)?

29. Why is it said that there will never be a blacksmith's forge in Cullen, Co. Cork?

30. Who was miraculously fed by birds, like the Old Testament prophet Elijah?

31. What is a martyrology?

32. What did the dragon of Glennawoo say when it ate all the wildlife in Lough Talt?

33. Approximately what percentage of saints in the medieval Irish martyrologies are female?

34. Who is especially known for miraculously creating ale?

35. Angels built a road for a family of sisters in Co. Cork. How many sisters were there?

36. Who was determined not to be 'sorrowful'?

37. Name as many Irish female saints who went to Cornwall as you can!

38. Traditionally, how many sisters did St Patrick have?

39. When Buriana was kidnapped, the King said that he would only release her if he miraculously heard the call of which bird (at the same time as it snowed)?

40. Name three saints who pulled out their eye(s)!

41. Who is the patron saint of western Norway?

42. Who travelled everywhere with a white cow?

43. Who had a lovely little donkey, which was badly treated by some people?

44. What is an anchoress?

45. Which Irish female saint name appears more often than any other in the martyrologies (and what does it mean)?

46. What does 'Kildare' mean?

47. What happened to Mad Crosbie (and why)?

48. What are the patients in Geel, Belgium called?

49. Who made Baron O'Fialain's castle disappear down into the ground?

50. Who is patron saint of Valentia Island, Co. Kerry?

51. What is a crosier?

52. Who were the 'Culdees'?

53. Whose bees turned into soldiers?

54. What did St Cainer see on fire in her vision? (Clue: it appeared the tallest of its kind in Ireland).

55. Whose flower is the dandelion?

Answers

1. Brigid of Kildare
2. Ia
3. Gobnait
4. Lupait
5. She was covered in slime and shells after she swan halfway down Ireland! Hence, she was called 'garb', meaning 'rough'
6. Faber
7. Skáld
8. A boat
9. Dáire
10. An eel bit onto his private parts and wouldn't come off until he repented to St Samthann!
11. Geel, Belgium
12. You will never die by drowning, and you will go straight to heaven.
13. Dahalin
14. Cainer
15. Tertullian
16. Killing and eating sheep and lambs!
17. Lí Ban
18. Fiesole, Italy
19. Cuman

20. Four
21. Íte
22. Brónach
23. Samthann
24. Sunniva
25. They turned to thirteen stones.
26. Bega
27. Fanchea
28. Grimonia and Proof
29. The forge was cursed by Lateerin because the blacksmith told her she was pretty!
30. Bega
31. A calendar of saints.
32. 'Delicious'!
33. 12 per cent
34. Brigid of Kildare
35. Three
36. Brónach
37. Ia, Buriana, Breage, Piala
38. Five
39. Cuckoo
40. Brigid of Kildare, Cranat, Darbiled
41. Sunniva
42. Brigid of Kildare
43. Íte

44. A female who, for religious reasons, withdraws from secular society to focus on her religion
45. Lassar/Lassair etc.
46. 'Church of the oak'
47. He developed rabies and lost his sanity because he disrespected a holy well, by putting his dogs in it!
48. 'Boarders'
49. Faber
50. Dar Erca
51. A bishop's staff
52. A group who wanted to be close to God and get back to the basics of Christianity
53. Gobnait
54. The round tower on Scattery Island, Co. Clare
55. Brigid of Kildare

Conclusion

Well, some of this was strange,
But no stories would I change,
Sadly, we're at the end,
We haven't just turned a bend!

Let your creative juices flow,
Line your pencils in a row,
Write and draw to your heart's content,
What the best bits of these stories meant!

Who were your favourites in this book?
Flick back through and take a look,
Why did they impact you so?
Cast your mind to and fro!

Try some poems like those I've made,
Whatever you write will be top grade,
Think and paint just how you feel,
Your unique creations are just the deal!

Glossary

Abbess: the head of an abbey or convent of nuns.

Acrostic: a poem where the first letter of each word spells out another word e.g. the five letters of the Greek alphabet, I-ch-th-u-s mean 'fish'. It spells out the first letters of Jesus Christ God's Son Saviour (in Greek).

Anchoress: a female who, for religious reasons, withdraws from secular society to focus on their religion e.g. to pray more.

Annals: a record of events year by year.

Apologist: someone who explains Christianity to those who don't believe.

Archaeological excavations: studying ancient civilizations by digging for the remains of their buildings, tools etc. and examining them.

Aristocratic: from a high ruling or privileged family; members of the nobility.

Arranged marriage: the bride and groom are selected by individuals other than the couple themselves, e.g. their parents. Sometimes a professional matchmaker might be used.

Artefact: an object made by humans, especially one from the past that is studied by archaeologists.

Bard: a professional storyteller, poet, music composer, and one who records family ancestry. They would have worked for a king or nobleman. Lower in importance to a filí poet.

Beltane: One of the four Gaelic seasonal festivals, along with Imbolc, Lughnasa and Samhain. It is the Gaelic May Day festival.

Bride price: money, property (or other form of wealth) paid by a groom (or his family) to the woman or the family of the woman he will be married to.

Bullaun: a stone that has an impression (hole) in it, which is often filled with rainwater. Some people believe the water has healing properties.

C: short for 'circa', a Latin word meaning 'about' or 'around'.

Caldera: a large cauldron-like hollow or depression that forms in a volcano when the magma chamber collapses.

Chalice: a cup in the shape of a goblet used for drinking the wine (or grape juice) in the Eucharist (or Mass).

Chasuble: the outermost liturgical vestment worn by clergy for the celebration of the Eucharist/Mass/Communion (bread and wine).

Church planter: someone who starts new churches.

Communion: bread and wine eaten and drunk, to remember Jesus' sacrifice on the cross.

Community: a group of people with something in common.

Convent: a community of nuns.

Convert: to change someone's religious beliefs to your beliefs.

Crosier: a staff, which is a symbol of the governing office of a bishop.

Culdees (Céilí Dé): a reform movement, wanting to go back to the basics of Christianity. It literally means 'spouses of God' as they wanted to be close to God. They flourished approximately between 750-850 AD. It was centred on Tallaght, near Dublin and led by the eighth-century monk, Máel Ruain.

Currach: an Irish wooden boat covered in animal skins.

D: short for 'died'.

Demon: an evil spirit.

Dynasty: a line of rulers or powerful people all from the same family.

Eucharist: bread and wine eaten and drunk, to remember Jesus' sacrifice on the cross.

Feast day: a day dedicated to a particular saint, when that saint is remembered and celebrated.

Filí: a high-ranking poet in Ireland (a higher rank than a bard).

Forced marriage: one or both of the couple are married without their consent or against their will.

Ford: a shallow place, usually to cross a river. They occur naturally, but may be constructed by people.

Foundress: a female who founds/starts something e.g. a convent/church/monastery.

Gael: the Irish.

God-fearing: respecting God.

Gospels: the four books containing the Christian message (Matthew, Mark, Luke & John).

Haiku: A short poem type originally from Japan. It is usually 3 lines long. e.g.

old pond
frog leaps in
water's sound

Hagiographer: the person who has written a Life (or Vita) of a saint.

Hagiography: another word for a Vita. A biography, often in Latin of a saint (about their life).

Hermit: a person who lives in seclusion, either by themselves or with a small number of others.

Hermitage: a type of convent or monastery.

Imbolc: One of the four Gaelic seasonal festivals, along with Beltane, Lughnasa and Samhain. It marks the beginning of spring.

Itinerant: travelling from place to place.

Lapdog: not a specific breed, but a general term for a type of dog that is small in size and friendly towards humans (so can sit on your lap).

Latin: the language of the Romans.

Limerick: a poem (usually funny and often rude) with five lines. The rhyme is AABBA. The first, second and fifth lines rhyme. The third and fourth lines share a different rhyme.

Martyr: a person who is killed because of their religious or other beliefs.

Martyrology: calendar of saints e.g. the Martyrology of Tallaght.

Merrow: a mermaid or merman in Irish folklore.

Meteor: known as a shooting star or falling star. It is a glowing meteoroid, comet or asteroid passing through earth's atmosphere.

Monastery: a community of monks, and possibly nuns.

Noble: from a high ruling/privileged family; aristocratic.

Nocturns: A prayer service celebrated by Christians at night.

Oratory: a place of worship (from the Latin verb 'orare', to pray).

Patron saint: a saint to whose protection a person, society, church or place is dedicated.

Paten: a small plate, usually made of silver or gold, used to hold Eucharistic bread which is to be consecrated during the Eucharist (or Mass).

Pattern day: a celebration of a patron saint's feast day.

Pilgrimage: a journey to search for spiritual (or new) meaning.

Prophecy: There are two parts to prophecy in the Bible. 1. Foretelling (communicating what God says will happen in the future e.g. Attracta predicted her brother's church would fail) and 2. Forth-telling (communicating what God is saying about the present, often with visual illustrations e.g. Fanchea got her brother to touch his tonsured head to stop him using violence).

Relic: part of a deceased holy person's body or belongings.

Revere: to honour a saint (the same as to venerate).

Rosary: a set of prayers used in the Catholic Church.

Round tower: a type of early medieval stone tower in Ireland. In Irish it is called a 'Cloigtheach', 'bell tower/house'. They were landmarks for visitors, bell towers (as their Irish name suggests), on occasion storehouses and places of refuge in times of attack!

Royal: the immediate family of kings and queens.

Saint: a person who is recognised as having an exceptional amount of holiness, likeness or closeness to God. They are Christians who are in heaven after death.

Samhain: One of the four Gaelic seasonal festivals, along with Imbolc, Beltane and Lughnasa. It marks the end of the harvest season and beginning of winter.

Selkie: mythological beings capable of changing from seal to human form by shedding their skin. In folklore, sometimes they intermarry with people (e.g. with the fisherman who caught them).

Tonsure: the practice of cutting or shaving some or all of the hair on the scalp, as a sign of religious devotion or humility.

Venerate: to honour a saint (the same as to revere).

Vestments: special garments (clothes) used in worship in some churches.

Vita: a biography in Latin of a saint (about their life). Only four Irish female saints have a Vita written about them (Brigid of Kildare, Íte, Moninne and Samthann).

197

Bibliography

Arbuthnot, Sharon and Ní Mhaonaigh, Máire and Toner, Gregory. *A History of Ireland in 100 Words*. (Dublin: Royal Irish Academy, 2019)

Arbuthnot, Sharon. *Wonders and Legends of Lough Neagh*. (Newtownards: Ulster Historical Foundation, 2021)

Finn, Clodagh. *Through Her Eyes: A New History of Ireland in 21 Women*. (Dublin: Gill Books, 2019)

Fish, Sarah. *'The Female Saints of Cornwall'*. (MA diss., Department of Welsh and Bilingual Studies, University of Wales, Trinity St David)

Irvin, Fr. Joseph. *Folk Tales of St Brigid*. (California, USA: CreateSpace Independent Publishing Platform, 2013)

Johnston, Dr. Elva. *'Íte: Patron of her People?'* (Peritia 14 (2001) 421-28)

Johnston, Dr. Elva *'Powerful Women or Patriarchal Weapons? Two Medieval Irish Saints'*. (Peritia (15) 2001)

Keane, Colm and O'Hagan, Una. *The Book of St Brigid*. (Co. Waterford: Capel Island, 2021)

Kissane, Dr. Noel. *Saint Brigid of Kildare: Life, Legend and Cult*. (Dublin: Four Courts Press, Open Air, 2017)

Mac Coitir, Niall. *Ireland's Animals: Myths, Legends & Folklore*. (Cork: Collins Press, 2015)

Mac Coitir, Niall. *Ireland's Bird's: Myths, Legends & Folklore*. (Cork: Collins Press, 2015)

Mac Coitir, Niall. *Ireland's Trees: Myths, Legends & Folklore*. (Cork: Collins Press, 2015)

Mac Coitir, Niall. *Ireland's Wild Plants: Myths, Legends & Folklore*. (Cork: Collins Press, 2015)

McBride, Doereen. *Fermanagh Folk Tales*. (Dublin: The History Press, 2015)

Mikaelsson, Prof. Lisbeth. *'Locality and Myth: The Resacralization of Selja and the Cult of St Sunniva'*

Martyrology of Donegal, www.archive.org

Martyrology of Gorman, www.archive.org

Martyrology of Oengus, www.archive.org

Martyrology of Tallaght, www.archive.org

O'Corrain, Donncha and Maguire, Fedelma. *'Irish Names'*. (Dublin: The Lilliput Press Ltd, 1990)

O'Hanlon, John Canon. *Lives of the Irish Saints, 9 volumes.* (Dublin: J. Duffy, circa 1875) – also available at www.archive.org

O'Hara, Dr. Alexander. *'Constructing A Saint: The Legend of St Sunniva In Twelfth-Century Norway'. Viking and Medieval Scandinavia, Vol. 5* (2009), pp. 105-121, Brepols, 2009)

O'Hara, Dr. Alexander. *'Death in the North: Norway's Irish Saint'.* (Death and the Irish: A Miscellany, ed. Salvador Ryan, Dublin: Wordwell, 2017)

Ó Riain, Prof. Emeritus Pádraig. *A Dictionary of Irish Saints* (Dublin: Four Courts Press, 2011).

⊗ Other sources consulted

https://archive.org/details/martyrologyofoen000oerg/page/160/mode/2up

https://brookstonbeerbulletin.com/beer-saints-st-brigid/

https://celt.ucc.ie/

https://www.duchas.ie/en

https://en.wikipedia.org/wiki/Alliterative_verse#Hrynhenda

https://en.wikipedia.org/wiki/Hallfre%C3%B0r_vandr%C3%A6%C3%B0ask%C3%A1ld

https://experience.arcgis.com/experience/9b31e05c1b744154b4584b1dce1f859b

https://fr.wikipedia.org/wiki/Grimonie_de_La_Capelle

https://fr.wikipedia.org/wiki/Preuve_de_Laon

https://holywellscorkandkerry.com/

http://irisharchaeology.ie/2020/08/irish-names-for-wild-birds/

https://www.logainm.ie/en/

http://www.megalithicireland.com/Scattery%20Island%20Round%20Tower,%20Clare.html

http://www.museumsofmayo.com/ionad-deirbhle/saint-deirbhile.html

http://www.omniumsanctorumhiberniae.com/

https://www.orielarts.com/songs/amhran-na-craoibhe/

https://orthochristian.com/116654.html

https://pilgrimagemedievalireland.com/

https://terreceltiche.altervista.org/amhran-na-bealtaine/

https://www.woodlandtrust.org.uk/blog/2019/04/identify-bird-song/

Acknowledgments

Special thanks to Michele Ainley (of @OmniumH for answering all my questions for 9 months), Sharon Arbuthnot (of @eDIL_Dictionary for the words in Old Irish), Sister Edel Bannon, Andreas F. Borchert, Emma Breadon, Rose Brennan, Amanda Clarke, Jim Dempsey, Dirk Desmet, Mary Dolan, Pascal Downing, the Embassy of Ireland in Norway, Rev. Becky Gibbs, Dr Loïc Guyon, Mark Joyce, Hanne Krogh, Dmitry Lapa, Frank McHugh (of Boho Heritage Organisation), Tamlyn O'Driscoll McHugh, John Mulqueen, Brian Nolan, Dr Louise Nugent, Gerry O'Callaghan, the late John Canon O'Hanlon (I couldn't have written my book without his wonderful 9 volumes of work), @placenamesni (especially Dr Frances Kane and Dr Mícheál Ó Mainnín), @poetryireland team, Dr Celeste Ray, Maura Reilly, Kennedy Roberts, Chris Robson, Doug Sim, Mike Sinclair, Prof. David Stifter (of @ChronHib), St Buryan PCC, Ann Ward.

Also, my sister, Heather Jackson (for being my taxi), my sister-in-law, Denise (not only did she give feedback on every story but she printed out all my research and stories on her printer) and my nephew, Matthew Jackson, for his outstanding illustrations!

Finally, everyone at Columba Books, Art Director Alba Esteban, and my publisher Garry O'Sullivan for giving me this opportunity and thinking of the name of the book title!